Katherine Howard

A play

William Nicholson

Samuel French — London
New York - Toronto - Hollywood

KATHERINE HOWARD

First performed at the Chichester Festival Theatre on the 9th September 1998 with the following cast:

Henry VIII	Richard Griffiths
Katherine Howard	Emilia Fox
Thomas Culpeper	Julian Rhind-Tutt
Anne of Cleves	Selina Griffiths
Thomas Howard, Duke of Norfolk	
	Denis Quilley
Thomas Cranmer, Archbishop of Canterbury	
	Jonathan Coy
Lady Jane Rochford	Frances Tomelty
Sir Thomas Wriothesley	Roger Booth
Mrs Mary Hall	Rachel Lumberg
William	James Benson
Captain of the King's Guard	Andrew MacDonald
Ladies in Waiting	Sarah Beckett
	Lucy Chalkley
Page/Soldier	William Buckhurst
Servants/Guards	Renata Champion,
	Jo Horstead, Becci Pritchard,
	Amy Stacy, Anna Walton,
	Chris Gibbs, Dominic Godfree,
	Adie Luff, Luke Osborne,
	Sam Tazzyman, Ben Thompson,
	James Thorpe

Directed by Robin Lefèvre
Designed by Liz Ascroft
Lighting designed by Mick Hughes

CHARACTERS

Henry VIII; 50

Katherine Howard: Henry's fifth wife, and niece of the Duke of Norfolk; 18

Thomas Culpeper: Katherine Howard's lover; 20s

Anne of Cleves: Henry's fourth wife, a German; 25

Thomas Howard, Duke of Norfolk: leader of the Catholic faction; 60s

Thomas Cranmer, Archbishop of Canterbury: leader of the Reformist faction; 50s

Lady Jane Rochford: Queen's lady-in-waiting; 40s

Sir Thomas Wriothesley: Privy Councillor, Reformist faction; 50s

Mrs Mary Hall: a chatterer; 20s

William: Cranmer's private secretary

Captain of the King's Guard

Menservants/Guards/Courtiers

Maidservants/Ladies of the court

The action of the play takes place in the royal palace between 6th January 1540, the wedding night of Henry VIII and his fourth wife, Anne of Cleves; and 13th February 1542, the execution of his fifth wife, Katherine Howard

Other plays by William Nicholson published by Samuel French Ltd

Map of the Heart
Shadowlands

ACT I

The royal palace. 6th January 1540. Night

There is a curtained pavilion C

When the play begins the stage is in darkness and the pavilion's front curtains are open. The king, Henry VIII, kneels at prayer, accompanied by his favourite, young Thomas Culpeper. One of Henry's legs is heavily bandaged from thigh to calf, but this is not noticeable at this stage. Henry and Culpeper are, as yet, unlit

We hear the sound of voices chanting the Mass

A procession of courtiers, and servants carrying candles, enters from either side

The Lights come up inside the pavilion to reveal Henry and Culpeper. The members of the procession kneel and the Mass proceeds

Henry completes his prayers, rises, and, assisted by Culpeper, makes his way off

The Lights go down inside the pavilion and the front curtains close

The courtiers rise and process off and the chanting comes to an end

A fanfare sounds. The curtains on the pavilion draw back and the Lights come up on the whole stage. A handsome royal bed is revealed in the pavilion. In the bed, bolt upright, sits the new queen, Anne, a German. She wears a nightgown, and her hair falls loose over her shoulders. She is rigid with apprehension. On either side of the bed, equally motionless, stand her two ladies-in-waiting: Lady Jane Rochford, once a beauty, no longer young, and Katherine Howard, eighteen years old, and charmingly lovely

A second procession now enters, and makes its solemn way towards the pavilion. In the lead is the Captain of the King's Guard, followed by his men; then the Duke of Norfolk, an aristocrat of the old style, leader of the Roman Catholic faction; then Archbishop Thomas Cranmer, leader of the Reformist faction, in sober black, with Sir Thomas Wriothesley, whose subdued costume shows that he too inclines towards reform. After them comes Henry, assisted by Culpeper. Henry wears a nightgown over his vast bulk, and moves with difficulty. His bandaged leg is now more obvious. Two Servants bring up the rear

Henry is not happy, and cares very little who knows it. When he is in sight of the ladies in the pavilion, but not yet in earshot, he stops, and gives vent to a long groan. The procession stops, in delayed reaction, ahead of him

Henry Do you love me, Thomas?

Culpeper You know I do, sir.

Henry Then do it for me, eh? She's a virgin, they tell me. You like virgins, don't you?

Cranmer (*turning back, smiling with anxiety*) We should proceed, sire. The people wait to celebrate tonight.

Henry It's all right for them. They don't have to share her bed. (*He gives another groaning sigh, and waves for the procession to continue*) Have you smelt her, Thomas? She stinks of rancid butter. Virginity does that. They have to be uncorked before they're twenty, or something curdles inside.

The Captain, at the procession's head, now reaches the pavilion, and comes smartly to attention. The Duke of Norfolk bows to the new queen. The protocol of the royal wedding night proceeds in formal style. Anne watches from the bed in bewilderment

Norfolk His royal majesty greets his gracious queen, and begs of the unquenchable love he feels for her pure and honoured person, that he may share with her the godly joys of matrimony on this his wedding night.

Lady Rochford Her royal majesty the queen receives the king's suit with rapture in her heart, and places her person humbly at his disposal, on this night and all succeeding nights.

Norfolk Captain.

The Captain of the Guard steps forward and raises his sword. First he holds the blade upright, and salutes the King

Captain Your majesty. (*Saluting Anne*) Your majesty. (*He thrusts his sword deep into the bed with a blood-curdling yell*)

Anne jumps with fright. No-one else seems to think the Captain's behaviour unusual, so she says nothing

(*Sheathing his sword and bowing to Norfolk*) The royal bed is purged, your grace.

Norfolk (*bowing to Henry*) The royal bed is purged, your majesty.

Henry (*turning to Anne*) Madam. With your permission.

Anne What? Oh! Yes.

The coverlet is drawn back by Lady Rochford and Katherine Howard and Henry climbs into the bed, with some difficulty. He sits there, beside Anne but not touching her, as stiff as she is. Cranmer, the Archbishop, now steps forward

Cranmer May Almighty God bless this union of his beloved children, Henry and Anne. May the joys of this night bring forth in due season the fruitful issue for which two nations pray. In Jesus's name. Amen.

There is a fanfare and the curtains close over the pavilion. The pavilion Lights fade

The procession makes its formal exit

The Lights fade to night

Thomas Culpeper enters, and paces in the darkness, clearly waiting for someone

Katherine Howard enters, carrying a candle. She goes to Culpeper, stepping softly, and they kiss. They speak in low voices

Culpeper Blow out the candle.

Katherine Then we'll have no light.

Culpeper We don't need light. (*He takes the candle from her and blows it out*)

Katherine moves into Culpeper's arms, and they kiss again, more intensely

Isn't that better?

Katherine So long as you're here.

Culpeper You're not afraid of the dark, are you, Kate?

Katherine Sometimes. Not now.

Culpeper The dark's kind to us. It takes away the unkind world. Look — no palace. No king. No family, or duty, or God.

Katherine Shush, Tom. Don't say such things. I don't want there to be nothing.

Culpeper Nothing can be anything, Kate. Anything we want. What do you want? A summer day in the countryside? A quiet river winding through fields of corn? You and me ...

Katherine Could it be winter?

Culpeper You want winter?

Katherine White frost over the land. Red sun rising.

Culpeper There it is. The dawn light turning the white world rosy. Just for us.

They stand together gazing at their imaginary world

Katherine When I was young, in Horsham, I would go to my window every morning when I woke, and if there was a clear sky I'd dress quickly, and hurry out into the park, and run towards the big red rising sun. It seemed so near.

Culpeper It's as near as you want it to be. This is our world.

Katherine Does the grass crackle when we step on it?

Culpeper Yes.

Katherine Does our breath smoke in the air?

Culpeper Yes.

Katherine And when I go back into the big dark lonely house, will I find you?

Culpeper Yes.

Katherine (*taking him in her arms*) We'll kneel in front of a fire together.

Culpeper I'll kiss your icy cheeks until they're warm again.(*He kisses her cheeks*)

Katherine Oh, Tom. I wish you had been there.

There is the sound of approaching footsteps. Katherine and Culpeper separate hastily

It'll be Jane. Don't let her see you.

Culpeper slips away to hide himself

Lady Rochford enters, carrying a candle

Lady Rochford Kate? In the dark?

Katherine My candle blew out.

Lady Rochford lights Katherine's candle from her own

Lady Rochford You should be in bed. You know the king will be up for Mass at six, wedding or no wedding.

Katherine I'm not tired.

Lady Rochford Not tired? Oh, I suppose you have a rendezvous with Culpeper.

Katherine How did you know?

Lady Rochford Good Lord, my dear, you didn't think it was a secret, did you? Thomas Culpeper is good enough in his way, but don't let him take liberties with you. I hope you know how to say no.

Katherine Yes, of course.

Lady Rochford It's a little word, but for a girl your age it's as good as a suit of armour. Kiss him, by all means. Bed with him. But if he asks you to marry him, the answer must be no.

Katherine Oh no, he wouldn't ask that.

Lady Rochford That's what all you girls think. But men are all the same. They only want one thing: an advantageous marriage. You belong to one of the first families in the land, Kate.

Katherine But I have no fortune.

Lady Rochford And the boy would like to marry money, of course.

Katherine Of course.

Lady Rochford Ah well, then, you're safe. Congratulations. Quite by chance, and at an unusually young age, you seem to have fallen into the most suitable circumstances for a love affair. All the charm and none of the danger. (*She sighs, remembering her youth*) Ah, well. I have no rendezvous, so I shall go to bed. Good-night, my dear.

Katherine Good-night.

Lady Rochford exits

Culpeper emerges from hiding

Culpeper Will she tell your uncle?

Katherine No. Jane can keep a secret.

Culpeper She's right. You must marry well. But you're to go on loving me.

Katherine Whether I want to or not?

Culpeper You want to, Kate. You know you want to.

Katherine I might. And then again, I might not.

Culpeper No lady's refused me yet.

Katherine Then go to your ladies. You don't need me.

Culpeper No, I don't *need* you. Anne Bassett is prettier, and richer ——

Katherine Have her. Everyone else at court has.

Culpeper So why am I creeping down dark corridors in the middle of the night to meet you?

Katherine Insomnia, I expect. Try warm milk and brandy.

Culpeper Why am I only easy when I'm with you?

Katherine I don't know, Tom. It's beyond comprehension.

Culpeper Tell me you'll go on loving me after you're married. I want to hear
you say it.

Katherine You're so vain! You don't want me. You just can't bear to think
of some other man having me.

Culpeper What other man? Tom Paston?

Katherine You see!

Culpeper Tom Paston has made a bet he'll have all six of the new queen's
maids of honour, in order of seniority ——

Katherine What do I care for Tom Paston? Just because he has the best legs
at court ——

Culpeper I challenge that! His thighs are positively fat! Are my thighs fat?

Katherine My sweet fool. Why do I love you so much?

Culpeper So you admit it?

Katherine I've loved you since I first saw you. I'll love you as long as I live.

Culpeper And after?

Katherine What? You want more?

Culpeper More, and more, and more.

Katherine (*taking his arm*) Come on. It'll be morning soon.

Culpeper I wish it were our wedding night.

Katherine Let's not wish for what we haven't got. Let's wish for a warm bed,
and you in my arms, and the night not over yet.

They exit, arm in arm

The Lights come up: it's early morning

A fanfare sounds

*The procession of the previous night enters: the Captain of the King's
Guard with drawn sword, the Archbishop of Canterbury, the Duke of
Norfolk, Sir Thomas Wriothesley, Thomas Culpeper, Lady Jane Rochford,
and Katherine Howard. The procession advances to the pavilion*

*The fanfare reaches its final flourish, the pavilion curtains are drawn back
and the pavilion Lights come up. There on the great royal bed sit Henry and
Anne, looking very much as they did the night before*

Henry Well, well. About time.

Cranmer I trust his majesty passed the night well.

Henry Well enough. Now get me out. No, I want Culpeper. Where's my
Thomas?

*Culpeper comes forward and lends his arm to Henry. At the same time the
ladies-in-waiting, Lady Rochford and Katherine Howard, take up their
places by Anne*

Norfolk May I express the dearest wish of all his majesty's loyal subjects, that the joys of his wedding night are the commencement of a greater joy, and that in due course her majesty will present the nation with a prince?

Henry Why not? The mother of God managed it, so why shouldn't she?

Henry climbs out of bed, leaning on Culpeper's arm. He turns to Anne and bows

Madam.

Anne inclines her head

The procession re-forms, minus Lady Rochford and Katherine Howard, with Henry bringing up the rear on Culpeper's arm

Filthy business, this sleeping in other people's beds. The poor do it in their poverty, and the beasts in their bestiality, but I'm the king. You'd think I'd be allowed to sleep alone.

Cranmer I believe some very well-born people sleep with their wives, majesty.

Henry Really? Who? Norfolk doesn't, he told me so. He has a little laundry maid who comes to his bed, but only for as long as it takes.

The procession exits, leaving Anne with Lady Rochford and Katherine in attendance

Anne speaks with a German accent

Anne Are they gone?

Lady Rochford Yes, your majesty.

Anne Then I shall rise.

The two ladies help the Queen to rise, and proceed to dress her for the day

Lady Rochford Your majesty passed the night comfortably?

Anne Oh, yes. More so than I had been expecting. You know, Lady Rochford, you will laugh at me, but I had been a little bit fearing of the king. The wedding night, you know. One gets such fearing ideas into one's head.

Lady Rochford I cried myself to sleep the night I first lay with my late husband.

Anne Did you so? That is terrible. Was he so unkind?

Lady Rochford The pain, ma'am. I was not ready for him.

Anne The pain?

Lady Rochford Your majesty felt no pain?

Anne No. I did not.

Lady Rochford But the king did honour your majesty with his — his conjugal attentions?

Anne Naturally he did. He put one hand on my body, like this. *(She places a hand on her breasts)* He touched me, like this. *(She moves her hand down to feel her stomach)* And so we slept.

A silence

Lady Rochford Nothing else, your majesty?

Anne What else should there be? Is this not enough?

Lady Rochford and Katherine shake their heads

Anne *(sighing)* I knew it was too good to be true.

Lady Rochford Did your mother not tell you of the duties of marriage, ma'am?

Anne She told me my husband was obliged by God to do a terrible thing to me, and I must endure and think of the sufferings of Christ on the cross.

Lady Rochford But she did not tell you what the terrible thing was?

Poor Anne shakes her head

Would your majesty like to know?

Anne *(looking at Katherine)* Do you know this thing, Katherine?

Katherine Yes, your majesty.

Anne Then I had better know too. *(She composes herself in the posture of one who expects to receive bad news)* Proceed.

Lady Rochford Your majesty will know that for any of nature's crops to grow, a seed must first be sown in fertile ground.

Anne Yes ...

Lady Rochford Our Creator has so ordained that woman is the fertile ground, and man the sower of the seed.

Anne I see.

Lady Rochford Your majesty will have observed that male animals differ from female animals.

Anne I have so observed.

Lady Rochford Sometimes, beneath the belly of a male horse, for example, there appears a — a sort of pipe.

Anne *(delighted to be following the clues so well)* I have seen it!

Lady Rochford Very good. Men too, your majesty, have just such a pipe.

Anne Are you sure?

Lady Rochford Perhaps your majesty has seen little boys at play in the river? In summer?

Anne (*searching her memory*) Yes ... But there were no pipes. A sort of little tassel, I think ...

Lady Rochford That's it, your majesty. A very good description. A little tassel. This tassel performs the work of the seed drill, ma'am ——

Anne No, no, Lady Rochford, you must be mistaken. A tassel cannot be a drill. It is too gentle.

Lady Rochford It grows fierce, ma'am.

Anne So!

Lady Rochford And just as the seed-drill is driven into the soft yielding soil, so does this angry extremity come close to defenceless womanhood and —— — (*She makes a quick stabbing gesture*)

Anne jumps

Anne Where?

Pause. A rapid look from Lady Rochford. Anne misses it; tries to repeat the look; gets the wrong destination. Lady Rochford repeats her look, playing out the pantomime. Anne copies her. And so gets there at last

Ah.

Pause. Anne composes herself

It is not for us to question the unknowable mind of God.

Lady Rochford No, ma'am.

Anne When I consider all these things, I find I think more highly of the human race. Clearly in order to carry out God's will, we are called upon to suffer, and this we do willingly and repeatedly, men and women alike. For see how many babies are born.

Lady Rochford The men do not suffer, ma'am.

Anne Do they not?

Lady Rochford They like it.

Anne They like it?

Lady Rochford It gives them pleasure, ma'am.

Anne How very odd. What sort of pleasure?

Lady Rochford I have absolutely no idea.

Anne The king did nothing of this sort with me last night.

Lady Rochford Then there will be no prince, ma'am.

Anne Ah.

Lady Rochford And there must be a prince, ma'am.

Anne Ah.

Lady Rochford But there is time. The king will return to your majesty's bed.

Anne He will? And he will drill me? Oh, blessed Jesus! Does it take long?

Lady Rochford Happily, ma'am, no. No longer than it takes to say a single Hail Mary.

Anne says the prayer, and the other two dutifully join her. All three instinctively speed up as it goes along, ending in a gabble and a rush, as if to get the terrible act over with as quickly as possible

Anne Hail Mary, full of grace ——

Anne
Lady Rochford *(together)* — the Lord is with thee. Blessed art thou amongst women and blessed is the fruit of thy
Katherine womb, Jesus. Holy Mary, mother of God, pray for us sinners, now and at the hour of our death. Amen.

All three release their breath together, in a single sigh of relief

Anne Well, ladies. We must be brave, and do our duty. Shall we go down?

They exit

The pavilion curtains close and the pavilion Lights fade

Henry enters, followed by the members of his Privy Council, Norfolk, Cranmer and Wriothesley

Cranmer It's an official arrangement, sire. A matter of state. One does not look for personal feelings when performing in one's official capacity.
Henry Am I to perform in my official capacity in the queen's bed, Cranmer?
Cranmer His majesty has risked his person on the field of battle for the honour of his country. He will not refuse to risk his person in the lists of love.
Henry Whoof, whoof, whoof.
Cranmer Sire?
Henry Empty breath, Cranmer. And pompous, if I may say so. Rather unlike you. Norfolk, you tell him.
Norfolk His majesty does not feel love for the queen.
Henry Does not. Can not. The fellow down there won't take orders, you know.
Cranmer You don't think, sire, that a little more time ——
Henry For what?
Cranmer You have only been married for one day, sire. Might not the view be taken that despair is still premature?

Henry I consider this so-called marriage a lie, a sin, and an abomination. Would you have me wade daily deeper into the mire? I am not married, do you hear? In the eyes of God, this is no marriage.

Cranmer But Germany ——

Henry I will not fornicate for Germany!

Norfolk If I may speak for his majesty. He is not in debate with his Privy Council, he is merely stating a fact. He is not married. Our job is to discover why.

Henry Exactly. Thank you, my wise old friend. I am the patient, you are the doctors. I tell you I am in pain, you seek out the cure. Excellent. I feel better already. Let me know when you have the solution.

Henry exits

Norfolk (*turning to Cranmer with a look of satisfaction*) You're the theologian, your grace, not I. But surely this is a simple matter. No consummation, no marriage.

Cranmer No marriage, no queen. No queen, a vacancy in the king's bed. And you, my lord, have long taken pleasure in filling vacancies.

Norfolk He's his own master. He'll do as he pleases.

Cranmer He's the king. He'll do his duty for his country.

Norfolk Not this time. Your Protestant wife revolts him.

Cranmer He has no quarrel with her religion.

Norfolk You think not? You've heard him complain of her sour smell. That's the reek of reform.

Cranmer Better than the sweet sickly incense of Rome.

Lady Rochford enters, and stands waiting to one side

Cranmer That river is crossed, my lord, and the bridges burned. There's no going back.

Norfolk Those with faith, your grace, have been known to walk on water.

Cranmer bows angrily, and he and Wriothesley exit

Lady Rochford approaches Norfolk, silently waiting on his instructions. Norfolk is deep in thought. After a moment:

Norfolk So. How's the queen?

Lady Rochford As virtuous this morning as she was last night.

Norfolk You're sure of that?

Lady Rochford I have her word for it.

Katherine and Culpeper enter, far off, walking together, talking softly, but not displaying any undue intimacy

Norfolk (*following Katherine with his eyes*) That can change. You women have your ways.

Lady Rochford Some do. Some don't.

Norfolk Elaborate?

Lady Rochford The queen's a good woman, but she lacks experience, elegance, and allure. Like all Germans, she has the dress sense of a parcel. That can be remedied, of course. She's almost childishly eager to learn.

Norfolk Save yourself the effort. The king has instructed his council to undo the marriage.

Lady Rochford Already?

Norfolk The king is impatient. We have very little time. There'll be no more diplomatic marriages. Next time, it's for love.

Lady Rochford For love?

Norfolk So who's it to be? She must be pretty, she must be willing, and she must be ours. What do you say to my niece Katherine?

Lady Rochford Katherine? She's very young.

Norfolk The younger the better. Will she do? That's the question. What do you make of her, since she came to court?

Now Lady Rochford too turns to watch Katherine, considering her in this new light

Lady Rochford Charming. Impressionable. Modest in her ambitions. Almost entirely uneducated.

Norfolk Wilful? Proud?

Lady Rochford Not proud, no. Vain, definitely, but it's a rather touching vanity. The pretty child who expects to be admired.

Norfolk Sensible?

Lady Rochford Yes.

Norfolk What about the boy?

Lady Rochford There is an attachment.

Norfolk I can always have him posted to Ireland. Very well. Leave her to me.

Lady Rochford exits

Norfolk strolls forward to intercept the young couple

So there you are, niece.

Katherine (*curtsying*) Uncle.

Culpeper (*bowing*) Your grace.

Norfolk Good morning, Mr Culpeper. They say Ireland can be very wet at this time of the year.

Culpeper I know nothing of Ireland, sir.

Norfolk Yet. (*He smiles thinly at Culpeper, and puts an avuncular arm round Katherine*) Allow us a few moments alone, Mr Culpeper. Family matters.

Culpeper bows again, and exits

Norfolk Now, niece. We haven't talked in a while, have we?

Katherine You were so kind as to hear me recite the Lord's Prayer on my sixth birthday, uncle.

Norfolk Yes, well, well. The burdens of office, and so forth. Still, here you are, grown into a beautiful woman, and the talk of the court.

Katherine Oh, no, uncle ——

Norfolk Oh, yes, uncle. You are talked of, Kate, you are asked after. Men say, who will she marry?

Katherine I've heard none of this, uncle.

Norfolk Why should you? Your marriage is none of your business, not until it's settled. But it is my business, Kate. Your father is dead, and I'm the head of the family. Your marriage must advance our family, and our faith. You do understand that?

Katherine Yes, uncle.

Norfolk Now, I've been looking over some suitable husbands for you. You're a Howard, which is good. You're pretty, which is good. But you're penniless, which is bad. This limits the field to the already-rich, which means, of course, the more mature men. The Duke of Carrara, for example. They say he's not altogether deaf. Or possibly the Count of Seville. Do you speak Spanish? No, why should you? His last wife, from Bruges, I think it was, died before she was even moderately fluent.

Katherine Must I marry a Spaniard, uncle?

Norfolk Yes, Kate, yes. Politics, you know. And soon, I think. After all, your youth and beauty won't last. They must be traded at the very point of ripeness, and for the very best price. Once the fruit is handled, it bruises.

Katherine turns away, not wanting her uncle to see how angry this makes her

Norfolk (*seeming not to notice*) How shall you like Spain? Hot, they say, out in the sun. Not that that should trouble you. I believe the custom there is for the women to remain indoors. Dressed entirely in black.

Katherine I know it's not my place to question your choice, sir. But is there no politics in England?

Norfolk Is there no politics in England? Now there's a question for an
  innocent young maid to ask.

Katherine I am happy in England, sir.

Norfolk I don't see how that affects matters. But still, you ask an interesting
  question. Is there no politics in England? Well, of course, there's always
  ... No, no, impossible ... But then again, why not?

Katherine What, uncle?

Norfolk I've just had a sort of a notion — I hardly know whether to tell you
  ... Let me ask you this, Kate. If you set your mind to making a man want
  you, do you think you could do it?

Katherine What man, uncle?

Norfolk A very rich, very powerful, and very proud man. There's an art to
  these matters, I know. Do you have it?

Katherine I don't know, uncle.

Norfolk I wonder if there's more to you than you let on? I wonder if beneath
  that sweet smile there's a woman who knows what she's worth, and means
  to get it?

Katherine I know this is a matter in which I have no freedom, sir. Tell me
  what you want of me, and if I can do it, I will.

Norfolk Good. good. This is very good. Down to business, eh, niece? Here
  we are, then. The king can't abide the queen. Does that surprise you?

Katherine No, sir.

Norfolk He'll put her away, Kate. He'll marry again. Does that surprise you?

Katherine No, sir.

Norfolk Why shouldn't he marry you?

Katherine Me!

Norfolk Ha! You didn't follow me over that jump, did you? Why shouldn't
  you be queen, Kate? I'll tell you why not. Because the king doesn't love
  you. The thought of it hasn't so much as entered his head. But it could. And
  if he should come to love you, there's nothing in the world to stop him
  making you queen. He has no need of money. What he wants is beauty,
  youth, happiness, and fertility.

Katherine Me!

Norfolk There's a battle being waged for the soul of England, Kate. Here!
  Now! Archbishop Cranmer and his reformers mean to strip the glory from
  us, and dress us in drab, and tell us our prayers in German. But the Howards
  are the first family of the faith. We stand firm. The German heresies must
  be expelled. Whoever has the heart of the king has the soul of the kingdom.
  Marry Henry, Kate, and give us a Catholic England once more!

Katherine But sir, the king doesn't want me.

*Culpeper enters and waits in the background for Katherine to come free
again*

Norfolk I know the man. He pines for love. The bed business would be hard, of course. (*He spots Culpeper and presses his advantage*) But at least it wouldn't carry you off to Spain.

Katherine Uncle, I must have time to think about this.

Norfolk Think. By all means think. "Is there no politics in England?". The king is just fifty years old, but his health is very poor. He can't live another ten years. And then — a dowager queen, fabulously rich, and not yet thirty — you could take your pick of England's manhood. (*He kisses her hand*)

Norfolk exits

Culpeper moves to Katherine. She takes his hands in hers, and draws deep breaths to calm herself

Katherine I'm frightened, Tom.

Culpeper Your uncle is making plans for your marriage?

Katherine Yes.

Culpeper We knew it would come. Who's it to be?

Katherine My uncle is very ambitious. But his plan will come to nothing. I'll make sure of that.

Culpeper Kate, why anger your uncle? You must marry somebody. We'll go on loving each other.

Katherine You don't understand.

Culpeper What don't I understand?

Katherine We may not have much more time alone. Please, Tom, don't ask me any more. Will you do something for me? Now?

Culpeper Of course.

Katherine We can't be married. But we can exchange vows.

Culpeper Of course, but ——

Katherine Now, Tom, now. "I, Katherine Howard, do swear —— "

Culpeper Wait.

Katherine Let me say it! Before it's too late!

Culpeper I will, I will. But look. (*He takes a ring from his pocket, and shows it to her*) We have to have a ring.

Katherine takes the ring, amazed

Look inside.

Katherine tries to make out the engraved letters

Katherine What does it say?

Culpeper T, K. Thomas, Katherine.

Katherine I see it. T, K. And there's more. *Fidus* ...
Culpeper *Fidus ultra finis.* Faithful beyond the end. I'll not let anyone else
   have you.
Katherine Oh, Tom.
Culpeper There's a kind of fidelity that needs no marriage, Kate.
Katherine I know it. (*She puts the ring on her finger*)

Katherine and Culpeper hold hands, and exchange solemn vows

Katherine I, Katherine Howard, do swear that Thomas Culpeper is my one
   true love, now and for ever.
Culpeper I, Thomas Culpeper, do swear that Katherine Howard is my one
   true love, now and for ever. Amen.
Katherine Amen, my darling. Amen.

Henry and Anne enter, accompanied by a train of attendants: Norfolk,
Cranmer, Wriothesley, and Lady Rochford

Henry and Anne walk hand in hand, formally on display as a newly-married
couple. Henry's manners are exemplary. He is affable and courteous to his
queen, though there are signs that his leg is hurting him. As they approach,
Katherine sinks into a curtsy, and Culpeper bows low. The royal party does
not notice them at first

Henry I'm told you no longer burn your heretics in Germany, ma'am. A
   mistake, if I may say so. A heretic is a teacher — of error, but still a teacher
   — and the burning is his final lesson. The lesson is, "Don't teach heresy",
   and a fearful flaming memorable lesson it is. (*His eyes fall on Katherine,*
   but she means nothing to him, and he continues with his train of thought)
   So by this arrangement the man who in life taught false lessons, in death
   teaches a true lesson. I have no doubt that when he faces his Maker, this
   final act of witness to the truth is taken into account. Wouldn't you say,
   Archbishop?
Cranmer We can't know, your majesty.
Henry Of course we can't know. We surmise. God is merciful. I surmise
   that He looks on the heretic with a more kindly eye, after a burning. I would,
   if I were God. Therefore I consider a burning an act of mercy. This is
   theology, ma'am. I think it bores you.
Anne No, sir. It seems to be a most dangerous sort of study.
Henry It is, it is. How could it not be? It is our window into eternity. Men
   become giddy leaning out of it. Is that Culpeper? Thomas! Give me your
   arm. My leg begins to hurt me.

Culpeper goes to the King's side, and the royal party makes its way off

Four years ago this month I got this wound. Thrown from my horse, smack, dead. Two hours, dead. Ask Norfolk, he was there. But my work wasn't finished, so here I am, born again, you might say. Four years old! That's even younger than you, Thomas ...

The royal party exits. Norfolk and Katherine remain behind

Norfolk (*looking Katherine up and down with a professional air*) Well?
Katherine Uncle?
Norfolk Have you thought?
Katherine Uncle, the king doesn't even see me.
Norfolk Don't worry about the king. Make him believe that you love him — not the king of England, but Henry Tudor, fat Henry Tudor, old Henry Tudor; love that lonely ageing carcass, and he'll give you the world.
Katherine How am I to make him believe that I love him, sir, when I don't love him?
Norfolk You'll be advised. There are ways and ways. I don't say, love the king. I say, make him feel loved. Good God, girl, it's a work of charity, and not a hard one, he's not a leper. (*He claps his hands*) Hoy! Anyone out there?

A servant comes running

Find Lady Rochford. I want her here. Right away.

The servant bows, and exits at a run

Jane understands these things. Do exactly as she says. She's served three queens now, she knows how it's done. For myself, I'll only say this. The king believes in order. He loves an independent mind, and a lively spirit, but he expects and requires a submissive will. Whatever he says to the contrary, Kate: submission, submission, submission.
Katherine Uncle, I don't think I'm clever enough to pretend to be any other than I am.
Norfolk You don't know till you try. Don't be so sincere, it's unattractive.

Lady Rochford enters, followed by two maidservants, carrying a gorgeous gown

Norfolk Jane. I give you your pupil.
Lady Rochford Good. Take off your dress, my dear.

The maidservants unlace Katherine's dress during the following. Katherine is bewildered, but doesn't resist

Katherine Jane? You know about this plan?

Lady Rochford Yes, dear. Your uncle consulted me as to your suitability.

Katherine You think me suitable?

Lady Rochford You will be.

Norfolk I really think, you know, Kate, that we've heard enough of this self-doubt. The point is taken. Here are two veterans of court warfare telling you you'll do, so you'll do, you know, and that's that.

Katherine Yes, uncle.

Norfolk Good. That's the spirit. I shall leave you to your lessons.

Norfolk exits

Lady Rochford (*looking at Katherine with a professional eye*) Yes, good. Now the gown.

The maidservants proceed to put the gown on Katherine

Katherine I can't do this, Jane.

Lady Rochford Of course you can. If I was your age, I could do it. Your looks, my experience, and we'll make the perfect wife between us.

Katherine But the king doesn't know I exist.

Lady Rochford We'll soon change that. He may be the king, but he's also a man, and all men work the same way. Listen to me, child. It isn't difficult.

Katherine is unhappy with both the dress and the proposed plan. Lady Rochford realizes this, but chooses to ignore it. During the following, the dress is laced tightly

There are three arrows in your quiver. First, you have Desire. All men crave physical love. That is of little interest, and less duration. Second, you have Anxiety. All men fear rejection. That is useful. Third, you have Vanity. All men want what is just out of reach, that they can admire themselves for getting. That is invaluable. The sensible woman therefore proceeds as follows. She shoots her first arrow —— (*She inspects Katherine's growing decolletée, as the dress is laced ever tighter. She gives some small tweaks to the dress to enhance the swell of the breasts*) Yes ... Do remember to smile, my dear. The gentleman needs to be assured in advance that his wooing will be welcome, or he will not woo.

Katherine Men aren't such great fools as you think, Jane.

Lady Rochford Not fools, perhaps. But ... unawakened, one might say. So: you have brought your gentleman to the pitch of complacent desire. Now you shoot your second arrow. You remove yourself from his reach. Not too far; men are easily discouraged. Perhaps you accept a rendezvous, and fail to appear. He waits in vain. He begins to be anxious. You come at last, you are sweet. A smile, and you withdraw again. His anxiety grows. Again, you smile and withdraw. Repeat until all he thinks of is winning you. His anxiety peaks. You yield. He is flooded with relief. And heavens, how proud of himself he is! For you see, my dear, it all comes down to this: if you can make a man's good opinion of himself depend upon your kindness to him, you have him for life.

Katherine's gown is now fully laced. Lady Rochford dismisses the maidservants

The maidservants bob and exit

Lady Rochford (*submitting Katherine to yet another critical scrutiny*) Yes, it will do.
Katherine I know myself, Jane. I can't perform as you describe.
Lady Rochford Why ever not?
Katherine This is the king! How can I be easy before him?
Lady Rochford Ah, I understand. You're shy. Of course you are. Well, we can use that. Watch me. (*She steps a pace away from Katherine, and adopts a timid posture, eyes cast down*) You're very young. The king over-awes you. But at the same time, you long to look at him.

Lady Rochford sneaks a quick look, meets Katherine's gaze, and looks down again in confusion

You look. You're dazzled. You blush, you look down. But what you've seen makes you long to see more. You dare to look again. (*She looks up again, and again retreats in confusion*) It's really just a variant on smile-and-withdraw. I think it could do very well.

Henry enters, some way off, walking with Norfolk

Lady Rochford takes Katherine and positions her where the king will see her as he passes. Katherine finds all this humiliating

Lady Rochford Do just as I say, Kate. I guarantee you he'll take the bait.
Katherine I tell you, I can't.
Lady Rochford Hush, hush. Remember: look down.

Henry and Norfolk approach. Katherine stands stiff as a post, looking down. Norfolk pretends surprise at the sight of her

Norfolk Why, if it isn't Kate! Sire, allow me to present my niece, Katherine
  Howard.

*Henry looks at Katherine. She says nothing, and remains resolutely looking
down*

Henry Have I seen you before?
Norfolk She's one of the queen's ladies, sire.

Katherine remains stiff and silent

Henry Can she talk?
Norfolk Kate. Pay your respects to your king.

*Katherine looks up. She's angry at the way she's being used, and her anger
gives her courage*

Katherine Your majesty.

Henry is very surprised. Norfolk is outraged

Norfolk I said respect, young lady!
Henry Why do you look at me like that?

Katherine looks down again

  Look at me when I speak to you!

*Katherine looks up again. Henry sees the independence in her eyes, and is
astounded. Nobody looks at him like this*

  Just what do you think you're doing?
Katherine As your majesty commands.
Henry Did I tell you to stare at me? What am I, that you stare at me in this
  way? Am I a freak?
Katherine Forgive me, your majesty. (*She looks down again*)
Henry (*flying into a rage*) Did I give you permission to look away? I'm the
  king! How dare you stand before me and — and look — and — and not
  look ... Am I to be goggled at in this way in my own palace? Damnation,
  woman! Who do you think you are?

*Norfolk moves forward to defuse the situation, all too aware that his plans
have gone horribly wrong*

Norfolk She offends you, sire. I'll take her away. Come, young lady.
Henry No. Wait.
Norfolk (*his rage passing*) I'll see to it that she knows her place in future.
Henry Yes, yes. Let her alone. (*To Katherine*) So who are you?
Katherine My uncle's niece, your majesty.
Norfolk That's enough! (*Again, he moves to take Katherine away*)
Henry (*stopping Norfolk*) I said, let her alone. In fact, let us both alone. I'll
  talk to her.
Norfolk Sire, this is wilfulness ——
Henry Shoo, shoo. Off you go.

Norfolk steps back to stand by Lady Rochford

  (*Waving them both further off*) Alone, I said. Shoo!

Norfolk and Lady Rochford move further back still

  (*Speaking to Katherine more calmly now*) So, Norfolk's niece. Why do
  you look at me like that?
Katherine If I have offended your majesty I ask you to forgive me.
Henry I didn't say I was offended. Did I say I was offended?
Katherine No, sir.
Henry So answer my question. You stare at the king, the king wants to know
  why.
Katherine I can't say, sir.
Henry Can't say? All that staring, and you saw nothing?
Katherine I saw you, sir.

This answer strikes Henry as significant

Henry Me? You saw me? Not the king?
Katherine I don't understand, sir.
Henry Why not? It's not hard. I'm a king, but I'm also a man. Nothing
  strange about that. You saw the man, perhaps. Is that how it was?
Katherine Yes, sir.
Henry Very well. That's that sorted out. So what's your name again?
Katherine Katherine Howard, sir.
Henry That's it. Kate, he called you. Well, Kate. We will meet again.

Henry exits

*Katherine stands very still, unsure what has happened. Norfolk and Lady
Rochford move forward, and proceed to circle Katherine, glaring at her with
disapproval*

Norfolk That was quite an exhibition.

Lady Rochford I said, look down. She stared. I said, be timid. She was brazen.

Norfolk I've a mind to pack her off to a nunnery.

Lady Rochford You don't seem to understand, Kate. You're one of the little people. You do as you're told.

Norfolk (*roaring at her in rage*) Do you understand?

Katherine Yes, uncle.

Norfolk Very well. (*He becomes calm again*) What do you think, Jane? Do we still have a chance?

Lady Rochford It's not out of the question. One thing we can be sure of: he won't forget her.

Norfolk So what do we do?

Lady Rochford Nothing. If there's to be a next move, it must come from the king.

Norfolk, Katherine and Lady Rochford move towards the exit

Norfolk Tell the girl how she's to respond, if it happens. (*To Katherine*) You, you listen! You do as you're told.

Lady Rochford Just remember what I said before. Smile and withdraw. Smile and withdraw.

Norfolk, Katherine and Lady Rochford exit

Henry enters, with Cranmer and Wriothesley

Henry I have proof, Cranmer, material proof, my physicians will tell you. What do you say to nocturnal emissions?

Cranmer Nocturnal emissions, sire?

Henry Don't you see? This is the proof of non-consummation that we need.

Cranmer I don't entirely follow your majesty.

Henry It's simple enough, man. If I'd done the act with the queen, there'd be nothing left to emit.

Cranmer Ah, yes. I see.

Henry My physicians assure me that the one act precludes the other. Good, eh?

Cranmer Excellent, sire. However — the act is not everything. Marriage is a sacrament made of three parts. The will to marry. The public declaration of that will ——

Henry And the consummation. So here we have no consummation.

Wriothesley The consummation doesn't have to be immediate, sire.

Henry How long am I to wait? You think it gets any easier? You think when I'm a year older, and the German is a year uglier, I'll erupt in a flush of passion? I don't think so, sir. This is no marriage. Get that into your heads. I should know, I'm the husband. That is, I'm not the husband.

Cranmer It is undoubtedly the case that if the king were to be declared impotent ——

Henry I am not impotent!

Cranmer Of course not, sire. I was hypothesizing.

Henry Well, don't! Say the king is impotent and say bloody murder across the land. The peace and unity of this realm is sustained by the king's potency, Cranmer.

Cranmer Naturally, sire. But you understand this makes the case all the more difficult to prove. We must demonstrate that your majesty is potent in some instances, but not in others.

Henry Now you're on the road.

Cranmer More specifically yet, we must demonstrate that while potent in general, your majesty is not potent with the queen.

Henry That's just how it is. That's the beauty of the nocturnal emissions.

Katherine enters, and passes by, deep in thought

Henry sees Katherine, and at once loses interest in his ministers

Henry That's all settled, then. Go and do it.

Cranmer Sire, there are concerns ——

Henry I said go.

Cranmer Your majesty.

Cranmer and Wriothesley bow and exit

Henry (*turning to face Katherine*) Katherine Howard.

Katherine (*hearing him; surprised*) Your majesty's servant.

Henry Come here.

Katherine comes to Henry

Henry I have enough servants. I don't want another. May I call you Kate?

Katherine Yes, sir.

Henry Look at me again, Kate, as you did before. What do you see?

Katherine I see my lord the king.

Henry You see a fat old man with a stinking leg. Oh, I know. I know it all. Once I was beautiful, Kate. Before you were even born. Sweet Jesus, what a thought! May I tell you how I was then, Kate?

Katherine Yes, your majesty.

Henry I was slender as an arrow. Truly! I could dance all night, and up with the sun to hunt until I was the last man in the saddle. I had hair then, Kate, hair like red gold. I was the prince of the world, and loved by God. And now? As you see. (*He spreads his arms before her*) Where did he go? That beautiful prince. Shall I tell you? He's here, imprisoned in this mountain of flesh, and I can't release him. Only my death will let him go. Then, on another day, that glorious day when time shall be no more and the dead shall rise again, my prince will come walking towards me, on clouds, on sunbeams, his cheeks rosy again, his eyes bright —— (*He drops his arms and changes his tone, becoming more rueful as he returns to reality*) So there you are. Old, but not entirely a fool. They've put you up to entice me, haven't they?

Pause

Katherine Yes, sir.

Henry "Yes, sir"? Well, now. I didn't expect that answer. Norfolk, is it?

Katherine Yes, sir.

Henry A very able man. You are enticing, Kate. He's chosen well. Come here, then. Play your part.

Katherine No, sir.

Henry "No, sir"? Then how are we to get on? I'm willing, Kate. Lead the old man a dance. I'll be a performing bear, if I must. (*He does an ambling bear-like jig for her*) See? No pride. Or too much pride, I hardly know. I want you, Kate. What more can I say?

Katherine I don't know you, sir.

Henry What do you want to know? I can barely walk. My leg hurts me day and night. I hate my marriage. I hate my body. I smell. Do you smell me, Kate?

Katherine Yes, sir.

Henry Then you're the only soul in the kingdom who does. I see their faces, you know. How they catch a whiff of it, and their eyes pop, and they start to smile as if it's all the perfumes of Arabia. As soon as I see that smirk I know who's downwind of me. I've grown used to it myself, of course. What's it like?

Katherine Like rotten meat, sir.

Henry Well, that's what it is. So if I disgust you so much, I don't see how this enticing is to be made to work. Norfolk won't be pleased with you, my dear. What will you tell him?

Katherine How I went to the king, and the king was kind to me, and showed me respect.

Henry Oh, that's not enough, Kate. He'll want you in my arms, if not in my
bed. We should have at least one kiss, my dear, for Norfolk's sake.
Katherine Let me know you better first, sir.
Henry Know, know, what is this "know"?

Katherine lifts her eyes and studies his face

(*Becoming uncomfortable*) Always looking, aren't you? Well, two can
play at that game. (*He stares into her eyes, and falls silent. Slowly his
agitated manner subsides into calm*)

It is as if a spell has fallen on them both. After a long, long moment:

Henry Do you know me better now?
Katherine Yes.
Henry What have you seen?
Katherine As your majesty said. I saw the man.
Henry Ah, Kate. (*He looks at her in quietness for another moment. Then all
at once he breaks away*) Damn, damn, damn! I'd give my soul to be young
again! I'd rip this old body off me if I could, but it clings like mud. Off! Off!
(*He pulls at his garments and beats his own body with his hands*) Chained
by every limb, shackles bolted to the very bones. Leave me, old brute! Old
fool! Get away! Foul stinking parasite, let me go! (*The burst of self-
violence leaves him exhausted. He stands there, panting, head bowed, his
clothes in disarray*) No strength left, you see? No breath. No escape. No
escape. (*He takes hold of Katherine's hand*) At least pity me.

Katherine tries to draw her hand away, but Henry will not let her go

I'd give you anything, Kate. Anything you ask.
Katherine Speak to my uncle, sir. He has the selling of me.
Henry Proud, Kate, proud. Prouder than I am. No-one's seen me as you see
me now. No-one. The king is shamed before you.
Katherine Why shamed, sir? We deal in truth. There's no shame in truth.
Henry (*releasing her hand; sighing*) If only it were so.

The king's two servants enter, bearing his robes of state

Henry spreads his arms to indicate that the servants should dress him

Katherine curtsies, backs away and exits

Henry watches her go all the way until she is gone. The robes are fitted around Henry and his mood and manner change once more. The imperious style returns

The members of the Privy Council enter and form around Henry: Norfolk, Cranmer and Wriothesley

Henry The king to his Council, concerning the German marriage. Firstly, the king is appointed by God, to further His will on earth. Secondly, men's bodies are created by God to perform the marriage act. Thirdly, the king cannot do the marriage act with the German queen. Therefore fourthly, either the king is not divinely appointed, or this is no marriage. (*He glares at his council, daring them to disagree*) You will convey my views to the convocation of bishops.

The members of his council bow their assent. Only Cranmer dares voice doubts

Cranmer Your majesty would surely not suggest that, as king, he is unable to act against God's will?
Henry Why not?
Cranmer The Creator has given all men free will, sire. And the king, being superior to all other men, cannot be less free.
Henry Nor am I. What are you driving at, Cranmer?
Cranmer That you are divinely appointed, sire, but not divinely controlled. We can't presume that it is God who makes you unable to perform the act with the queen.
Henry Why not? Isn't God all-powerful?
Cranmer Indeed so, sire, but ——
Henry God can make me do the act with the queen, if He so wishes. But He does not make me do the act with the queen. Therefore He does not wish it.
Norfolk That's clear enough, I should think.

Cranmer sighs, and gives up

Cranmer The convocation will give the matter the most careful, and respectful, thought, majesty.
Henry Do that. Take your time. The will of God in this matter must be probed to the very bottom. I expect an answer by the end of the week.
Cranmer The end of the week! I don't think ——
Henry (*turning his withering stare on to Cranmer*) I don't ask you to think. Pray, Archbishop. Make your mind receptive to the will of God. It doesn't take long.

Cranmer Yes, sire.

Henry Then get on with it. Trot-trot. Off you go. (*He shoos Cranmer and Wriothesley out*) Norfolk. A word.

Cranmer and Wriothesley exit, bowing as they go. Norfolk stays

Henry What's happened to Cranmer? He used to be faster on his feet than that.

Norfolk He's for the German alliance, sire.

Henry There is no German alliance. When the marriage is declared null and void, so is the alliance. I don't think that breaks your heart.

Norfolk No, sire. I see nothing to be gained from Germany. Too many little bits and pieces.

Pause

Henry I like her, you know.

Norfolk Sire?

Henry Oh, come on. We've known each other long enough, you and I. She's not like the rest of them. Your niece, man. Katherine Howard.

Norfolk I was afraid she might turn out a little too high-spirited, sire.

Henry No, no. As I say, I like her. But I don't know if she likes me.

Norfolk How can she not, sire? You're her king.

Henry Well, that's the thing, you see. She doesn't entirely see me that way.

Norfolk (*shocked*) She has no right ... I beg your pardon, sire. I shall speak to her about this, never fear.

Henry Hush, hush. Leave her alone. I don't want her frightened off.

Norfolk No, sire, but respect. Obedience. Submission.

Henry Leave her alone. This is my last chance, old friend. Don't you think I don't know it?

Norfolk exits

Henry is alone. He stands gazing at the gathering dusk. He speaks his thoughts aloud

Henry Respect. Obedience. Submission. Whatever man strives for in this world, I have. Whatever I want, I need only name it, and it's given me. No, not given: it's mine already. The giving of it is no gift. This is what God must feel. Creation is His, we are His, how can we not adore Him? There had to be a Lucifer. There had to be a serpent in the garden, Adam had to fall from grace, or how could God find love? It seems a hard bargain. The human race, every man and woman from Adam to me, cast out of Eden into this hurting world, all so God can be loved. And did it work, I wonder? Is God content now?

Katherine enters, behind Henry

Henry hears Katherine enter, but does not turn round. He speaks low, as if he fears he may be just imagining her

Henry Kate?
Katherine Sir.
Henry I've been philosophizing. Did you hear me?
Katherine No, sir.
Henry Just as well. (*He turns to her*) Not dark yet. Come closer.

Katherine comes closer

I love theology. Logic, mystery, terror, sublimity. I love the light of reason, and I dread the dark.
Katherine You should call for lights, sir.

Henry smiles at that: a simple practical approach to the problem

Henry So I should. Soon. Do you mind?
Katherine No, sir.
Henry Our Lord and Saviour Jesus Christ lived thirty-three years on this earth. For thirty-three years now I've been king. In all that time, my will alone ... I want you to kiss me, Kate, but I'll not ask it. As soon as the words are out of my mouth they become commands. So I don't ask you to kiss me. I don't ask for your kindness. Here I stand, not asking. You shall do as you please.
Katherine No, sir. I'm too poor to do as I please.
Henry And too proud. Everyone's so damn proud. I've had enough of pride. I just want to be happy. How's the smell, by the way?
Katherine Better.
Henry I had my physician put on two extra layers of binding. So — how are we to get on?
Katherine As you wish, sir.
Henry As I wish? If only it were so. (*He turns to watch the dying of the day*) I don't wish the day to end, but it's ending. The sun goes down, and the light fades from the sky, and mankind is delivered into darkness. Do you know what I wish then? Nothing. After grief, after despair, comes — nothing. Desirelessness. That's a tunnel down to hell. So I must have light, light,

more light! There it goes. Down, down, down. Stay with me tonight, Kate.
I'll not be afraid with you by me.

Katherine No, sir.

Henry Do I disgust you?

Katherine No, sir.

Henry Well, then. Since you must do this trade with somebody, why not with
me?

*Henry leans down to kiss Katherine, and she lets him. He kisses her with
unexpected gentleness. Tears come to her eyes, and she turns away from him.
He sees the tears, and brushes her cheeks softly*

Yes, it's a bad business, I know. Does the old monster defile you?

Katherine I felt you tremble as you kissed me.

Henry I do tremble. Already I start to be afraid of losing you.

Katherine Have you got me already, sir? What was the price?

Henry I'll not buy you, Kate. I'll not command you. I'll woo you. But I have
to do my wooing like an old man. Young lovers show their beauty, old
lovers their needs. I'm afraid, Kate, and I'm alone, and I'm growing old.
I cry in the nights. It's a backwards kind of love-making, I know, but it's
still a gift of a kind. My need is my gift. You could make me happy, if you
would.

Katherine What am I to do, sir?

Henry Come to my bed tonight.

Katherine No, sir.

Henry Virtuous, Kate? I thought we were agreed your virtue was for sale.

Katherine At the right price, sir.

Henry Then name your price.

Katherine Honour.

Henry Ah! So you want to be queen? You're right. You're right. You know
your own value. That's good. Drive up the price, and up goes the value. I
suppose they told you to bargain this way. "Don't give in. Make the old fool
pay."

Katherine Yes, sir.

Henry Well, they're quite right, aren't they? They think of me as a spoilt
child, a child who throws tantrums and has to be placated. I'm to be petted
and given treats. I see it all, sometimes I want to laugh at them, but I take
the treats, Kate, I take them. I get tired. I can't fight everybody. But I do miss
candour. And that's what you have. You don't say much more than "Yes,
sir" and "No, sir", but it's your own truth each time, isn't it?

Katherine Yes, sir.

Henry So you would have me, if I were free?

Katherine Ask me when you're free, sir.
Henry Will you kiss me again?

Katherine kisses Henry, and this time he holds her close and clings to her. And they part. Katherine steps back from Henry, and looks at him for a moment

   Katherine exits

Henry stands staring at the last of the light

Henry (*low; to himself*) Save me, Kate. Save me from the darkness. (*He claps his hands and shouts*) Lights! Lights! Hoy, out there! Lights!

   He exits

   Anne enters, attended by Katherine. Anne is very jumpy

Anne Dignity, Kate, dignity. My mother taught me that. What will they do with me, do you think?
Katherine No-one wishes you any harm, ma'am.
Anne Stay close by me, Kate. I don't like this uncle of yours. He makes too many plans. Ah! Dignity!

Approaching footsteps are heard. Anne hears them and freezes into an attitude of regal composure

   Norfolk enters and bows, but not as fully as before

Norfolk I come from his majesty, ma'am. He wishes me to inform you that the convocation of bishops has pronounced judgement in the matter of your marriage. The marriage is declared null and void, ma'am. With the king's compliments, ma'am.
Anne I am divorced?
Norfolk No, ma'am. You are not married.
Anne But I was married, sir. I remember it well. You were there.
Norfolk That was the appearance of a marriage, ma'am. Now that the learned bishops have examined the matter, they find that you were not married after all.
Anne I'm sure the learned bishops understand these matters better than I.
Norfolk The king appreciates how much pain it must give you to be parted from him in this way ——

Anne *(alarmed)* Pain? Is there to be pain?

Norfolk No, ma'am, you misunderstand me. I refer to the ache in your heart, due to the natural love and affection you feel for your royal husband, as you believed him to be; mistakenly, as it now appears ——

Anne It was the wedding that put the idea into my head, sir.

Norfolk Quite so. It is the king's pleasure, in sympathy for your loss of his person, that henceforth you call yourself his sister.

Anne His sister?

Norfolk *(taking out some papers and referring to them)* As his sister, he settles on you for the duration of your life an annuity of £4,000. In addition he grants you the castle at Hever, and the manors of Richmond and Bletchingly.

Anne I'm to be a sister?

Norfolk May I tell the king that though as a woman your heart is heavy, as a loyal subject you accept the judgement?

Anne Oh, yes, do ... Heavy heart, quite; loyal subject, exactly so ... £4,000 a year, you said?

Norfolk Four — thousand — pounds — a year.

Anne And there's nothing more I have to do?

Norfolk Nothing, ma'am. Except bear your grief well, and learn to be happy without so gracious a lord.

Anne I will pray for strength, sir. Every single night.

Norfolk bows, and exits

Anne looks at Katherine wide-eyed. There is a moment of silence. Then she lets out a cry of sheer pleasure, and starts to dance about

Alleluia! I'm free! I'm rich!

Katherine bursts into laughter, delighted by Anne's joy. Anne takes Katherine's hands and dances her round and round

(Singing out) Four thousand a year! No more men! Four thousand a year! No more men! Four thousand a year! No more men! *(She comes to a stop, panting and laughing)* I'm to be a sister, Kate! Oh, I'm so happy. Men are all very well, but — so much noise. So many requirements. *(She embraces Katherine in her joy)*

Culpeper enters

Anne There is your young man. Go to him, Kate! Be happy, as I am.

Anne exits

Culpeper comes to Katherine's side. He is very agitated

Culpeper What's happening? I never see you. I hear impossible rumours.
Katherine Not impossible, Tom.
Culpeper How? How can it be?
Katherine I've tried to resist, but everything I do ... It's like a net that tightens around me. Don't blame me, Tom. I never asked for this.
Culpeper But — the king!
Katherine My uncle wants it very much.
Culpeper *(bitterly)* Of course he does.
Katherine Do you hate me?
Culpeper Hate you? How could I ever hate you? No ... But — the king!

But even as he speaks the shock of it is passing, and he can see from Katherine's face how she still longs for his love

Oh, my sweet Kate ... There'll be glory for you. You'll be the most beautiful of all his queens. And he'll love you, because there isn't a man living could fail to love you.
Katherine Oh, Tom ...
Culpeper You have to marry someone, so why not ... why not — the king? So I should be happy for you. And I am happy for you. And proud ...
Katherine *(deeply touched by his generosity)* My darling dearest Tom. *(She takes him in her arms)* We're the little people. Our lives aren't ours to command.

A servant enters at a run

First Servant *(shouting)* The king! Stand for the king!

Katherine and Culpeper separate

A second servant enters at a run

Second Servant *(shouting)* The king! The king! Stand for the king!

Culpeper exits in haste

Norfolk and Wriothesley come sweeping in, followed by Henry

Katherine curtsies

Henry Why does everybody have to shout wherever I go? Ah, Kate. There you are.

Katherine Sir.

Henry (*to Norfolk and Wriothesly*) All right, you can all go.

Norfolk, Wriothesley and the servants bow and exit, Norfolk giving Katherine a warning look as he leaves. Henry and Katherine are left alone

Henry Well, Kate. You've heard the news? The bishops have ruled.

Katherine Yes, sir.

Henry How does Lady Anne take it?

Katherine She resigns herself to the will of God, sir.

Henry I'm glad to hear it. And you?

Katherine Me, sir?

Henry Yes, you, you, you. I'm free now, Kate.

Katherine Yes, sir.

Henry Well?

Katherine Well what, sir?

Henry Damn it, you know what I mean. Do you want the full protocol? Shall I send Sir Thomas Wriothesley to the Duke of Norfolk to present draft terms for subsequent revision by both parties subject to later ratification? I'm the king, Kate, I have professionals do this sort of thing for me. I don't know what to say.

Katherine Tell me what you want of me, sir.

Henry You know what I want. I want you.

Katherine You want me for what?

Henry Damnation, Kate, you know what I want. I want you for my wife.

Katherine As your majesty wishes.

Henry No, no. Look here, Kate. This isn't an affair of state, this is just me, you understand, just you. You're young, beautiful, there's no reason why you should care for an ancient wreck of a man like me ——

Katherine Who is my lord and master.

Henry stops and looks at the ground, then at Katherine

Henry You won't flatter me, will you? You won't let the old man have his illusions. I won't order you, Kate.

Katherine From the king, even a request is an order. If you ask me, I will obey.

Henry Then I don't ask. I'll not have you marry me under compulsion.

Katherine is silent. They look at each other

What a damnable business it is being king! What are we to do?

Katherine You expect too much, sir.

Henry How do I expect too much? I don't expect you to be of royal blood. I don't expect you to bring me a large dowry. It seems to me that for once in my life my demands are within reason. How too much, Kate?

Katherine You're not a woman, sir. If you were a woman, you wouldn't expect the freedom to love as you please. A woman must serve her family.

Henry And I must serve the realm.

Katherine No, sir, you're free ——

Henry Free? Free? The king is the nation's slave. My every impulse of desire creates factions in the court. My love is turned to coin, my happiness changes hands at thirty percent before my smile has faded. I can't make a friend without him ending up Lord Chancellor. I can't go to bed with a woman without founding a dynasty. Free, Kate? Never! Never yet!

Katherine And yet your body is your own. If you were a woman, the most intimate parts of your body would be at the disposal of others.

Henry Well, so it is with me. I must be a woman.

Katherine No, sir. No man knows what it is to be a woman.

Henry So a woman can't love? Is that your conclusion?

Katherine No, sir. A woman can find love. But first, she must marry a man she hardly knows. She must allow him to use her body for his pleasure. She must give birth in pain, year after year, until her body is broken. She must live to see many of her children die before her. Through these years, if she is fortunate, the stranger in her house will slowly become her friend, and they will learn to be kind to each other, and to know each other well. Then after many more years, bound together by joy and suffering, he will die, and she will discover, missing the noises in the house, and the old familiar face, and the long habit of trustfulness, that this was love, sir, that this after all was love.

Henry Oh, Kate. Oh my Kate.

Katherine Don't blame me if I come to you under compulsion. What does it matter how we begin? Neither of us are free. Let's take each other for friends, like prisoners thrown into the same jail. And if we're kind to each other, the love will come.

Henry Kate, Kate. My sweet Kate. Where did you learn such things?

Katherine My mother died before I knew her. My father sent me away to live in the great house of my great relations, who cared nothing for me. A lonely child learns the way of the world young.

Henry As did I.

A silence. They look into each other's eyes

Very well. You reprove me. This longing to be freely loved is a vanity. I shall learn to be more humble. I'd un-king myself if I could, but ... The king wants you for his wife, Kate. Will you have him?

Katherine I am at his majesty's command.

Henry (*taking her in his arms*) Oh Kate, Kate. You child of truth. Never lie
to me. Never. You say it takes years, but I swear to you, Kate, I love you
now, in this moment, I love you now and I don't even know why. I'll work,
Kate, I'll work and study, I'll watch and listen, I'll learn to make you love
me. I'll be so good to you, sweetheart, we'll be such friends, and tell each
other everything in our hearts, until all I have is yours and all of me is in
you, and then you'll love me, Kate, I swear it, then you'll love me.

Henry kisses Katherine

*Servants enter with two royal capes, which are placed on Henry and
Katherine*

*The members of the court enter from each side, bowing to Henry as they do
so, assembling in formal array: Norfolk, Cranmer, Wriothesley, Lady
Rochford, the Captain of the Guard, the other Lords and Ladies — and
Culpeper. Culpeper carries off the moment of obeisance with proper respect*

The procession with which the play began re-forms. The fanfare sounds

Bright lights come up far US, indicating the distant palace

The procession exits, escorting the new royal pair into the palace

Curtain

ACT II

The pavilion curtains are closed; behind them is the royal bed

Music. Dancing couples sweep on to the stage

The members of the court enter backwards, applauding: Norfolk, Wriothesley, Cranmer, Lords and Ladies

Culpeper enters apart from the rest, and watches without joining in the celebrations

Henry and Katherine enter, dancing, both gorgeously dressed

The royal couple perform their stately circles, slowed down by the king's sheer weight, and by the pain in his wounded leg. The court applauds

Cranmer *(still clapping; aside to Wriothesly)* I've never seen the king happier. It's a complete disaster.
Wriothesley *(clapping)* Well, it's done now.
Cranmer What's done can be undone.

The music stops, and the dance comes to an end. Henry bows. Katherine curtsies. The courtiers clap. Henry, exhausted, motions for assistance, and a Servant comes to his side. Leaning on the Servant, he moves slowly towards the exit, joined by Archbishop Cranmer

Cranmer The queen looks well, sire.
Henry Why shouldn't she? She's young. And I'm young again, because of her, Cranmer. Not the body, the body is as you see, but within, in my heart, in my soul, young again!

Henry, Cranmer and the rest of the court exit except Norfolk, Lady Rochford, Katherine and Culpeper

Norfolk and Lady Rochford circle Katherine, as they did before, but this time clapping her softly as if she has just completed a bravura performance. In the background, Culpeper still watches and waits

Norfolk Bravo! You've done a superb job. Hasn't she been magnificent, Jane?

Lady Rochford Beyond everything. I never saw a man so besotted.

Norfolk I underestimated you, Kate. I admit it. Well played!

Lady Rochford Every move judged to perfection.

Katherine I judged nothing. I played nothing.

Norfolk And won nothing, eh, Kate? Who then is our pretty young queen?

Katherine Do you think the king would love me as he does because I played a game? He knows it's no game. He loves me because I'm true to him, and for that I honour him.

Norfolk and Lady Rochford respond with another round of applause

Norfolk Bravo! Bravo! I salute a master!

Katherine It isn't an act, uncle.

Norfolk Of course not. The sincere heart, the authentic spirit, the self forgotten for the self created, this is beyond acting, Kate, this is transfiguration!

Katherine turns away, angry and hurt

Norfolk meets Lady Rochford's eyes. Lady Rochford believes she understands the true source of Katherine's unease. Norfolk and Lady Rochford head for the exit, Lady Rochford pointing discreetly to her midriff

Ah, that. Yes, early days, early days. The king does the full honours, I hear?

Lady Rochford Every night.

Norfolk Then nothing to worry about there.

They exit

The Lights fade to a night setting

Culpeper sees Katherine is alone, and dares to approach her. Katherine becomes aware that he's near, but she's nervous, and won't look at him

Katherine You mustn't be seen alone with me.

Culpeper I'm leaving court. I've come to say goodbye. (*He's trying to hide the pain he feels, but his voice gives him away during the following*)

Katherine You're leaving?

Culpeper Yes. I must. It's for the best.

Katherine Oh, Tom ...

Culpeper I'm not as strong as I thought. Ever since your ... Ever since ... Life without you ... There is no life without you.

Katherine Please, Tom.
Culpeper I know. It's wrong to speak to you like this. I'm so unhappy, Kate. With you, everything. Without you, nothing.
Katherine *(low)* What can I do?
Culpeper I must leave. I know that. But before I go ——

Lady Rochford enters. She sees Culpeper and makes urgent shooing gestures

Katherine Go, Tom. Quickly.

One last pleading look, and Culpeper exits

Lady Rochford *(approaching)* The king's on his way. You will take care, won't you, my dear?
Katherine I'm not a fool, Jane.

Henry enters, accompanied by a servant with a candle

Lady Rochford *(curtsying)* Your majesty.
Henry Go away.

Lady Rochford curtsies again, and exits

(To the servant) You go too. I'll take the light.

The servant gives Henry the candle, and exits, bowing

That's better, eh? Just you and me.

Katherine takes his arm, and they stroll up and down, very much at ease with each other

Henry Ah ... You calm me, Kate. How do you do that?
Katherine I don't know, sir. I don't know how I do anything.
Henry That's it, you see. No calculation. No unseemly scrabbling for answers. I find that restful.
Katherine I'm happy if it pleases you.
Henry Do you see how the candle-light cares for us? It doesn't reach far at all, and yet it's always far enough, because it moves on ahead of us. Even if we go faster —— *(He moves faster, as if trying to overtake the candle-light)* See? No darkness for us. Always light ahead. This is a symbol, Kate. Our understanding is limited, but it's sufficient. Let's be content with that, eh?

Katherine What if the light were to go out?

Henry It won't. I'll be sure of that.

Katherine What if we were to blow it out?

Henry Blow it out? Why?

Katherine To see what it's like.

Henry See what it's like? We wouldn't see anything. It'd be dark.

Katherine Why should we mind about that?

Henry Is this a test, Kate?

Katherine No, sir. It's an adventure.

Henry An adventure?

Katherine If you don't like it, one call would bring a servant running with more light.

Henry True, true. (*He thinks about it*) All right. Let's try your adventure. (*He blows out the candle*)

Katherine What do you see?

Henry Not a damn thing.

Katherine What would you like to see?

Henry What would I like to see? I'd like to see England thirty years ago, and a misty autumn morning. My hunter being saddled in the yard. The hounds yelping. My huntsman banging on the door.

Katherine There it is.

Henry And you, Kate. I want you with me.

Katherine Here I am.

Henry By God, I smell the horses, and the steaming forest! I want to be away, with the hounds baying and the wind in my face! Will you wait for me? When the hunting's good, I'm gone all day.

Katherine I'll wait.

Henry I'll come back hot and happy and aching in every bone. Hungry as a hunter, as they say. That's the true keen hunger. Oh Kate, will you really be waiting for me?

Katherine I'm your wife, sir. Of course I'll be waiting.

Henry God bless you. God bless you. (*He embraces her*)

Katherine So how do you like your adventure in the dark?

Henry With you, I'd walk through the valley of the shadow of death and fear no evil.

Katherine Then a short passage in your own palace shouldn't be too hard.

They exit

The Lights come up on a daytime setting

Archbishop Cranmer's secretary William enters, accompanied by a plump young woman, Mrs Mary Hall. She is visibly excited by her grand surroundings

Cranmer enters

William presents the lady to Cranmer

William Mrs Hall, your grace.

Cranmer holds out his ring; Mary Hall kisses it

Cranmer Mrs Hall. Thank you for coming. You've had a long journey, I
think?

Mary Hall Yes, your grace. Though I've had longer. Which isn't to say that
your grace isn't right enough, a long journey, as you put it ——

Cranmer William, notes, please. William has told you why I wish to hear
what you have to say?

Mary Hall Oh yes, your grace, the goings-on, which I did speak about at the
time to her ladyship, being her ladyship's chamberer, and thinking it my
duty ——

Cranmer Why don't we start at the beginning, Mrs Hall?

Mrs Hall looks blank

William (*prompting Mrs Hall*) You shared a bedroom with the queen, before
she was queen. In the big house at Lambeth.

Mary Hall The queen, of course, your grace, Katherine Howard that was,
Kate, we called her, and Joan Bulmer, and Alice Restwold; we were all
such friends, your grace, ask Kate, she'll tell you the same herself for she
can't lie, sir, not to save her life, and no more can I, though there are times
when I don't think it wise to trouble Mr Hall ——

Cranmer The bedroom, Mrs Hall. You shared a bedroom.

Mary Hall So we did, the dormitory as we called it; I was in my bed here,
and Kate there, and we would lie in the dark and talk, oh, about everything
under the sun, though there was no sun to speak of, not at night, and when
her young man came to her I wasn't to say anything ——

Cranmer Her young man?

Mary Hall Mr Dereham, your grace, the tutor, a young man who thought
far too well of himself, in my opinion ——

Cranmer And this young man came to Katherine Howard, in her bed? You
saw him, with your own eyes?

Mary Hall So he did, your grace, just exactly as you say, and I was there,
and I saw him with my own eyes, as your grace so feelingly expresses it.

Cranmer And what, Mrs Hall, did you see?

Mary Hall Why, your grace, in he would come, and like this to me, "Hush!
Hush!", and creep to Kate's bed, and in through the curtains, and draw them

fast behind him, and there they would do as married folk do, your grace —
I don't know how else to say it.

Cranmer Curtains? There were curtains round the bed?

Mary Hall Yes, your grace.

Cranmer Lace curtains?

Mary Hall Oh no, your grace. Good heavy damask.

Cranmer What, then, Mrs Hall, did you see with your own eyes?

Mary Hall I saw him go in, your grace.

Cranmer And after that?

Mary Hall They did as I say, your grace, which was very wrong, for they
weren't married, and have never married yet, because Kate married the
king, you know, and is queen, which was the greatest surprise I ever had
in my life when Mr Hall told me, "Kate Howard queen!"; I cried ——

Cranmer Then how, Mrs Hall, do you know?

Mary Hall Know what, your grace?

Cranmer That they did as married folk do?

Mary Hall I could hear them, your grace.

Cranmer I see. And what did you hear?

Mary Hall Noises, your grace.

Cranmer What kind of noises?

Mary Hall Breathing noises, your grace. What you might call married
breathing.

Cranmer Mrs Hall, you are making the most serious allegation against the
moral character of the queen. It is absolutely essential that you provide
clear and unequivocal proof. We have established that you saw nothing.
What precisely did you hear?

Mary Hall It's not easy to describe, your grace. A sort of sighing.

Cranmer As I might sigh when I reflect on my sinfulness, and the Lord's
mercy?

Mary Hall Oh no, your grace. Like this. (*She proceeds to give a vivid sound
rendition of two people making love, taking both parts: a soft womanly
sigh, a more urgent manly sigh, a melting croon, a deep groan, a sudden
cry, heavy panting, ecstatic chirps, rapid breaths speeding to a climax, and
a last long dying moan*)

Cranmer and William gaze at her in awe

Cranmer Married breathing, Mrs Hall?

Mary Hall Yes, your grace.

Cranmer Very well. We will talk again. Tell no-one what you have told me.
These are grave matters. No-one at all.

Mary Hall Yes, your grace. That is, no, your grace.

Cranmer William. See Mrs Hall to her lodgings.

Mary Hall and William exit

Wriothesley enters

Cranmer The cracks begin to appear. What do you say to dissolute living? Fornication?
Wriothesley Before the marriage?
Cranmer If it were after the marriage, it would be adultery.
Wriothesley Adultery is better.
Cranmer Of course adultery is better. But fornication is all we have, so far.
Wriothesley Well, the king won't like it.
Cranmer The king doesn't know. Nor will we tell him.
Wriothesley I thought that was the point.
Cranmer The point, sir, is the salvation of Christ's reformed church in England. To achieve that, we must disempower the Roman faction. To achieve that, we must turn the king against his Howard wife.
Wriothesley He won't like fornication, though.
Cranmer Fornication before marriage is no treason. It's not even grounds for divorce. We have to have adultery.
Wriothesley I said adultery was better.
Cranmer To think that the service of Christ should bring me to this. Snuffling about in women's bedrooms like a spaniel in a whorehouse. I hate it. I find it petty and demeaning, and — in short, sir, that is why I do it. I'm a proud man, my vice is pride, and this is my penance. God tests us all, each in our fashion.

They exit

Culpeper enters. He paces back and forth

Lady Rochford enters, on her way to the queen's Bedchamber

Lady Rochford Mr Culpeper. Again.
Culpeper Lady Rochford.
Lady Rochford It won't do, you know.
Culpeper I know. I'm leaving court.
Lady Rochford This isn't the way to leave court. This is the way to the queen's bedchamber.
Culpeper *(low)* I must see her one more time.
Lady Rochford It's not possible, sir.
Culpeper One more time, and then I'll go. I promise. Surely you can find a way? *(Sensing her sympathy, he seizes Lady Rochford's hand and kisses it)* I'd do anything.

Lady Rochford Why, Mr Culpeper, how charming you are when you want something. But I don't see what I can do.
Culpeper Anywhere. Any hour. Day or night.
Lady Rochford Well, well. I shall speak to her. Go now. I hear them coming.

Culpeper exits

Katherine enters, accompanied by a maidservant

The curtains open on the pavilion and the Lights come up, revealing the royal bed, with Katherine's night clothes laid on it. Katherine stands still; the maidservant undresses her during the following. Lady Rochford moves to stand beside her

Lady Rochford Will the king honour us with his presence tonight, your majesty?
Katherine No, Jane. The king is gone to Greenwich.
Lady Rochford Of course. I had forgotten.

Lady Rochford moves behind Katherine and takes over the undressing from the maidservant, indicating to her with a look that she is to leave

The maidservant curtsies and exits

Katherine looks round in surprise, and sees that it is Lady Rochford who is now dressing her. Lady Rochford dresses Katherine in her night clothes during the following

Katherine You, Jane? Serving me?
Lady Rochford I wanted a word alone. About your friend.
Katherine My friend?
Lady Rochford He says if he can see you one more time, he'll go. I think you know, it would be better if he were to go.
Katherine Oh, Tom...
Lady Rochford It'll lead to gossip. He does dangle about so.
Katherine He wants to say goodbye.
Lady Rochford Don't think I'm blaming him, my dear. I find it all rather touching. But you must be careful.
Katherine Is there any way, Jane? Just a few moments alone together, the way we used to be?
Lady Rochford The way you used to be?
Katherine Just to say goodbye.
Lady Rochford There are servants everywhere. Except, of course ... (*She shakes her head*)

Katherine Except what?

Lady Rochford There is one place where you're alone. Here.

Katherine Here!

Lady Rochford No-one sees you in your bedchamber. Only the king, and the king is away tonight.

Katherine Is it possible?

Lady Rochford Who would know? Only me, and I know all there is to know already. If you wish, I could stand guard in the outer room.

Katherine Would you do so much for me, Jane?

Lady Rochford Your uncle is grateful to you. Call it a small repayment.

Katherine If we could meet as we used to meet, just once ... Just to say goodbye.

Lady Rochford To say goodbye, quite. This kind of arrangement is very common, my dear. The essence of it is discretion. So long as all concerned are discreet, there's no harm in it.

Katherine is now in her night clothes, ready for bed

Katherine Is he nearby?

Lady Rochford I can find him.

Katherine Very well, then, Jane.

Lady Rochford (*curtsying low to Katherine*) May I wish your majesty a good night.

Lady Rochford exits

Katherine goes towards the great bed. Then she moves away again, made restless by a nervous longing

Culpeper enters. He stands gazing at Katherine

Culpeper I like you better without all the jewels. You look like the Kate I used to know.

Katherine I haven't changed.

Culpeper Haven't you?

They look at each other in silence, remembering

Katherine When do you leave?

Culpeper In the morning.

Katherine I'll miss you.

Culpeper I'll miss you. No, why say that? The truth is, I don't know how I'll go on living without you.

Katherine Oh, Tom ...

Culpeper You see, even though there's no hope, it seems I still love you. Ridiculous, isn't it? In fact, I love you a great deal more.

Katherine (*distressed*) Please ...

Culpeper sees her distress. He speaks hastily, before she asks him to go

Culpeper Yes, I know, what's done is done, we must live the life we have and not the life we dream of. And you — you have a life of glory.

Katherine I never asked for it.

Culpeper Does he treat you well?

Katherine Yes. He's very kind to me.

Culpeper Kind? That's good.

Silence. Katherine knows exactly what he's thinking

Katherine You want to know, do I love him?

Culpeper I don't ask it.

Katherine I do. I ask it. I ask myself, am I such a child, that I'm dazzled by pretty things? How can I be happy when my Tom is unhappy?

Culpeper So you are — happy — with him?

Katherine Yes.

Culpeper watches her, and loves her, even as she denies him what he longs for

Culpeper You won't lie, will you? Not even to save me hurt.

Katherine Don't blame me. I've been so poor for so long, I've been so despised by my grand relations, and now to see them bow to me, and outdo each other to please me ... how can I not find that sweet?

Culpeper Of course it's sweet. And you deserve it.

Katherine And there's something else. I know I can make the king happy. I do make him happy. And that — I can only tell you how it is, in plain words — that makes me love him.

Culpeper You love him because you make him happy?

Katherine I know it's all backwards. I don't understand it. But that's how it is.

Culpeper Oh, Kate. What am I to do? Even when you tell me how you love another man, it makes me love you more.

Katherine We've always been true to each other, you and I. Nothing must ever change that.

Culpeper So — you love the king. And Culpeper?

Katherine And Culpeper too.

Culpeper You love us both?

Katherine It sounds wicked, I know. Or impossible. But it feels so natural to me. When I'm with the king, I love him. When I'm with you, I love you.

Culpeper And if you had to choose?

Katherine Choose? I get no choice. The bit is in my mouth. I go where I'm tugged.

Culpeper But just suppose that you could choose. In your dreams.

Katherine In my dreams? I choose you. Always you. Surely you know that? Haven't I made you a vow? Don't I have your ring? I'll love you as long as I live.

Culpeper And after?

Katherine And for ever.

Culpeper Then I can go.

Katherine The world's so big. There'll be others.

Culpeper But where am I to find another like you?

Katherine Not like me. Different in every way. There are so many ways of loving.

Culpeper Well, I shall do my best. But when it's all over, and I lay my weary body down, and my soul slips free at last, I shall come looking for you, Kate. And if I don't find you there before me, well, I'll just sit down quietly and wait for you.

Culpeper gives Katherine a last look, and exits

Katherine watches him all the way, until he's out of sight. Then she too exits

The curtains close on the pavilion and the Lights go down

Cranmer enters, and paces up and down, filled with frustration

William, Cranmer's secretary, enters

Cranmer Well?

William Nothing, your grace. None of her servants have seen her even touch another man. Not since she became queen.

Cranmer I don't believe it. The woman's a proven whore. There must have been adultery. It's because they know it's a hanging matter.

William If I could use instruments, your grace.

Cranmer I can't use instruments when I haven't got a crime. I need evidence. I need proof. (*He falls into intense thought*)

William I could always arrange some evidence, your grace. Just to start the ball rolling.

Cranmer Be quiet. I'm thinking ... Yes, yes. That's the way. After all, what is faith, but certainty without evidence? (*To William*) Very well. Send her in.

William moves to one side and beckons offstage

Lady Rochford enters

Cranmer holds out his hand. Lady Rochford curtseys to Cranmer and kisses his ring

Cranmer I am disappointed, Lady Rochford.

Lady Rochford Your grace?

Cranmer You have been entrusted with the most precious jewel in the realm. The queen's honour. I wish to establish your degree of guilt in this sad business.

Lady Rochford What sad business?

Cranmer You seem surprised. Is it possible you know nothing? In which case you are guilty of neglecting your duties. No small matter, ma'am, when the queen is so young. Would you put her soul in peril because you are too lazy to watch over her?

Lady Rochford I beg your grace to believe me, I do not neglect my duties. I never sleep till the queen sleeps, and when she wakes, I wake. This is unjust, sir.

Cranmer Then if you are not lazy, ma'am, you must be vicious. For if you know, why have you not spoken out? Why have you allowed the young queen to leave the narrow path of virtue?

Lady Rochford (*frightened*) I don't understand, your grace. What has the queen done?

Cranmer That is for you to tell me, ma'am. This is a test. Your true loyalty should be to the king. If you act now to protect the king's honour, we will overlook the fact that you have not come forward at the earliest opportunity. If you continue to be obstinate, we must conclude that you are complicit in the affair, and you will be judged accordingly.

Lady Rochford What affair, sir?

Cranmer Is that your answer?

Lady Rochford If you would tell me the nature of your suspicions ——

Cranmer I have no suspicions. I have knowledge.

Lady Rochford Then what need do you have of me?

Cranmer I have no need of you, ma'am. It is you who has need of me. Soon now all this will be made known to the king, and your part in it will be discovered. I offer you the chance to be among the accusers, rather than among the accused. There is no middle way. I will not help you. You must speak out now, of your own free will, or remain silent, and let the investigation take its course.

Lady Rochford *(bitterly)* Of my own free will? No, sir. There's no freedom here.

Cranmer Enough. I have too many calls on my time to wait on the wrigglings of your conscience. (*He turns to go*)

Lady Rochford Wait.

Cranmer stops

Please understand. I've grown fond of her. She's very young.

Cranmer That will be taken into account.

Lady Rochford What will happen to her?

Cranmer That's for the king to decide.

Lady Rochford And Culpeper?

Cranmer Culpeper?

Too late, Lady Rochford sees that he didn't know after all

Lady Rochford You didn't know?

Cranmer I know now.

Lady Rochford God forgive me.

Cranmer God won't forgive you for assisting the queen to commit adultery, Lady Rochford. Nor will the king.

Lady Rochford What was I to do? Forbid the queen to do as she chooses? Lock her in her room?

Cranmer Your simple duty was to tell the king, or his ministers. You did not do that. The penalty for abetting an act of treason is death.

Lady Rochford is shocked into silence

How many times has Culpeper consorted with the queen?

Lady Rochford Once, that I know of.

Cranmer Where?

Lady Rochford In the queen's bedchamber.

Cranmer And what did they do there?

Lady Rochford I don't know. I was in the outer room.

Cranmer Well, then, you're a woman of the world. What do you suppose a fine young man does with a beautiful young woman, in a bedchamber, alone? This is adultery, is it not?

Lady Rochford Yes, your grace.

Cranmer Very good. So you did know, after all.

Lady Rochford What will happen to me, your grace?

Cranmer That depends. If you continue to demonstrate this newly-discovered concern for the king, perhaps he'll be merciful when it comes to judgement.

Lady Rochford I'll do whatever you ask.

Cranmer Go back to the queen. Say nothing. You can't save her now. She'll be arrested shortly. If at any point in the days that follow she unburdens herself to you, you'll tell me what she says. We must have a confession. Do you understand?

Lady Rochford Yes, your grace.

Cranmer And tokens. There'll be love tokens. Letters, even better. Bring me some outward and undeniable sign of their love. A love token will silence any remaining doubts. And, ma'am, it will save your neck. That is plainly put, is it not?

Lady Rochford Yes, your grace.

Cranmer Leave me now. I must speak to the king.

Lady Rochford exits

Henry enters, from the hunt

Cranmer moves away, not wishing to intrude, but does not exit

Katherine enters, and comes to Henry

Henry Well, Kate! I stayed the course.

Katherine And made the kill, I hear.

Henry Yes, well, they managed it for me, you know. But the great thing is, I was there at the end.

Katherine (*laughing*) Your strength didn't fail you.

Henry Not once. Why are you laughing?

Katherine I was thinking of your horse. Lucky his strength didn't fail him.

Henry Well, it's true, the beast did all the work. He's a vast huge animal, Kate. Has to be, to carry me.

Katherine And a long way down if you fall.

Henry A terrible long way.

Katherine What a hero you are! To stay tied on to your great horse till they led you up a stag to kill! (*She laughs even more*)

Henry Oh, Kate, you revive me. I was feeling almost weary, but now ... How is it you can laugh at me and I don't mind?

Katherine I don't know. I never know anything.

Henry I'll tell you what it is. You do me the honour of not taking me for a fool. Of course I know I make a spectacle of myself, lumbering after the field. But you're the only one who says so. You speak as you find, Kate. and that's rare.

Katherine If I'm easy with you, sire, it's because you're easy with me.
Henry There you are. I talk and talk, and you say it all in a word. Easy. Yes, my Kate. We are easy with each other, aren't we?

Henry kisses Katherine

Katherine Oof! You smell!
Henry The smell of the chase. Sweat and leather. No more rotten meat.
Katherine I shall order you a hot tub.
Henry I'll sleep in it.
Katherine Do as you please in it, so long as you wash.

Katherine exits

Henry looks after her, shaking his head and smiling. Cranmer approaches him

Cranmer Your majesty?
Henry She's a jewel, Cranmer. A bright jewel. I've been hunting! Can you believe it? Well, I must go and scrape off the mud. (*He lumbers towards the exit*)
Cranmer (*hurrying after Henry*) Your majesty ——
Henry Well?
Cranmer How am I to act in this new matter?
Henry What new matter?
Cranmer Ah, I see that I have been wrong to trouble you, sire. (*He makes to withdraw*)
Henry (*stopping*) What are you talking about?
Cranmer Forgive me, sire. I supposed you had been told. I was eager to place my convictions at your service. I believe the rumours to be untrue. This is malice at work, sire.
Henry What malice? What rumours?
Cranmer If the rumours are false, what is to be gained by spreading them? The true target of this malice is your peace of mind, sire. I will not do the work of your enemies.
Henry What enemies?
Cranmer I shall root them out, sire.
Henry Are these rumours to do with the queen not being with child yet?
Cranmer No, sire. The queen ... No, sire. Nothing of that sort.
Henry The queen? There are rumours about the queen? What sort of rumours?
Cranmer Absurd tales, sire. Beyond believing. The queen is not capable of deceiving you, sire.

Henry Not capable of deceiving me how?

Cranmer Let someone else be the messenger, majesty. That is not my trade.

Henry You're the first in line, Cranmer, so you'll have to do. Come on, out with it.

Cranmer The rumour is of the lowest kind, sire. That the queen has deceived you with another man.

Henry That's impossible, Cranmer. She hasn't a deceitful bone in her body. Moreover, to lie with another man, to put in question the parentage of any subsequent child — it's treason, it's insanity, she would never do it. What other man?

Cranmer I will not accuse where I have no evidence, sire.

Henry There you are. No evidence. Why does anyone credit this nonsense? You don't, do you?

Cranmer No, sire. I am all the more sure this is a fabrication, sire, because the same tattlers tell tales of the queen's former life, at Lambeth. Of liaisons, and lovers, and every kind of moonshine. We know that to be false, sire, because the queen came to your bed a virgin.

Henry Of course it's nonsense.

Cranmer A man of your experience, sire, knows when he is first in the field, or when he follows where others have beaten a path.

Henry Of course I do. A little earthy for a man of God, Cranmer.

Cranmer I wish only to point out to your majesty that all the evidence points to the queen's innocence.

Henry doesn't speak for a long moment

Henry As it happens, there was no blood.

Cranmer Not all virgins bleed, sire.

Henry Nor timidity. Nor pain. She gave me great joy, Cranmer. She was — comfortable.

Cranmer Happy the man whose wife is his comforter.

Henry Yes ...

Katherine enters

Katherine They're waiting for you, sir. They boil kettles, and the water cools, and they boil them again. Pity the kettles, sir.

Cranmer bows and exits

Henry looks at Katherine, and his faith revives

Henry What nonsense it all is.

Katherine What, my lord?

Henry There's bad doings afoot, Kate. Cranmer's been telling me you have lovers all over the land.

Katherine That's a lie! A wicked lie! The Archbishop means to hurt me, sir.

Henry No, no, he's not so stupid. He's only passing on the gossip. He doesn't believe it himself.

Katherine Then why does he tell you?

Henry I need to know these things.

Katherine There are no lovers, sir. You are my husband and my lord. Since our marriage, no other man has touched me.

Henry I know it, Kate. I see it in your eyes.

Katherine We must keep faith in each other, sir. I'm surrounded by those who'd destroy me if they could.

Henry I have faith in you. I love you, Kate. If I were to lose you, I would have no more will to live. I've known many women, Kate, you know it, and I've married some of them. But you're the first has loved me with open eyes.

Katherine Trust me, sir. And go and wash.

Henry kisses Katherine, smiling, and exits

Lady Rochford enters. She tries to conceal her agitation

Katherine Jane, someone is spreading lies about me. That I have lovers. Have you heard this?

Lady Rochford There's always talk at court.

Katherine The lies have reached the king. He doesn't believe them, of course. Cranmer is behind it all. I must speak to my uncle.

Lady Rochford Is there to be an investigation?

Katherine Investigation? What is there to investigate?

Lady Rochford I only ask, because once before, when similar accusations were made — the first Queen Anne, that is — there were investigations.

Katherine Let them investigate. I have nothing to hide.

Lady Rochford Then we needn't worry. Only sometimes, people keep mementoes — letters, for example — that might be misunderstood.

Katherine What letters?

Lady Rochford Well — from a former close friend, perhaps.

Katherine You mean Tom? No, Tom wrote me no letters.

Lady Rochford Then there is no danger.

Katherine I suppose it's Tom they name in these rumours.

Lady Rochford I believe it is.

Katherine Poor Tom. Thank God he's leaving court.

Lady Rochford And if he has kept any mementoes, he'd be well advised to destroy them.

Katherine What a worrier you are, Jane. We gave each other nothing. (*She remembers*) The ring! (*She unties a secret pocket and takes out the ring*) Tom gave me this. Before I was married, of course.
Lady Rochford A ring is innocent enough.
Katherine It has T, K, inside. And some Latin. *Fidus ultra finis*. Faithful beyond the end.
Lady Rochford That could be misunderstood.
Katherine What should I do?
Lady Rochford Don't leave it here, child. There might be a search.
Katherine I shall bury it in the garden.
Lady Rochford And be seen? And have it dug up?
Katherine What then can I do?
Lady Rochford Give it to me. No-one watches me. I'll find a safe place for it.
Katherine Oh, do please, Jane. I don't want Tom to get into any trouble because of me. (*She hands Lady Rochford the ring*) Go now. And thank you. You're a true friend.

Katherine exits

Lady Rochford studies the ring

Cranmer enters

Lady Rochford I have what you wanted. (*She gives him the ring*) Look inside.
Cranmer (*looking inside the ring*) Good. This is very good. (*He studies the ring*)

Norfolk enters

Lady Rochford (*low; to Cranmer*) I look to you to protect me.

Lady Rochford exits, curtsying to Norfolk as she passes him

Cranmer *Fidus ultra finis. Ultra* takes the accusative, *finem*. The young are so ill-educated these days.
Norfolk (*coming up to Cranmer*) What have you done to Jane Rochford? She looks positively ill.
Cranmer We have a problem. You know the rumours about the queen?
Norfolk No.
Cranmer If you and all your faction are brought down, the whole court will be in chaos.

Norfolk Brought down? What's the girl done?

Cranmer What do you think? But you would push her at him.

Norfolk Who is it? Culpeper?

Cranmer nods

I'll kill him! Are you sure?

Cranmer (*showing Norfolk the ring*) T for Thomas, K for Katherine. He lay
with her in her own bedchamber this very week.

Norfolk I'll kill them both! Who says?

Cranmer Lady Rochford.

Norfolk How? How could she be so stupid?

Cranmer She's very young.

Norfolk Does the king know?

Cranmer He's heard the rumours. But he dismisses them, of course.

Norfolk You're right. This could be the end of the Howards. It could easily
be the end of me. When will you tell him? I need time.

Cranmer Perhaps I shouldn't be the one to tell him. Perhaps it should be you.

Norfolk Me?

Cranmer If you show yourself the most zealous in denouncing the treachery
— after all, it is a slur on the honour of your family ——

Norfolk It is that! And believe me, I feel it.

Cranmer Who better than yourself to purge the disgrace?

Norfolk Yes, yes ... Why this sudden concern for my well-being, Cranmer?

Cranmer My first duty is to the peace of the realm.

Norfolk (*smiling thinly*) Quite so.

Cranmer Of course, we may be too hasty in thinking the worst of the queen.
Perhaps we shouldn't trouble the king.

Norfolk He'll hear it soon enough. No, you're right. I must show that I place
king and country above family. I must be pitiless.

*A small procession enters: the Captain and men of the King's Guard,
followed by Henry, in full regal dress*

Norfolk throws himself on to one knee before Henry

Norfolk Your majesty, the shock! The horror! I knew nothing! This blow
strikes also at me, out of the very bosom of my own family — though the
plain truth is I hardly knew her, as anyone will tell you ... So young, and
so corrupt! Who would have thought it possible? A prostitute, sire, a lecher,
a monster of vice; I say it myself — let none say I shrink from the truth —
she must be burned, sire!

Henry (*staring at Norfolk in astonishment*) Burned, Norfolk?

Norfolk To have deceived you, sire, and me, and all the world — this is witchery. This is devil's work.

Henry turns his gaze on Cranmer

Cranmer There is some evidence, sire. Strong, but not conclusive.
Norfolk Say the word, majesty. I'll arrest them. Interrogate them. Try them. Burn them.
Henry Burning again, Norfolk?
Norfolk You may be confident that I will purge this evil to the very root.
Henry (*looking from Norfolk to Cranmer*) What is this evidence?
Cranmer It seems the queen received a visitor in the night, majesty. In her bedchamber. We have no evidence that they did anything illicit.
Norfolk Alone? In her bedchamber? At night?
Cranmer Then there is the ring.

Cranmer gives Henry the ring

Henry (*studying the ring*) T. Who is T?
Norfolk Thomas Culpeper, majesty. Her lover.
Henry Culpeper. (*He stares at the ring, breathing hard*) Culpeper gave Kate this ring?
Cranmer It appears so, sire.
Henry And she gave it to you?
Cranmer No, sire. To Lady Jane Rochford. To hide, now that suspicions have been aroused.
Henry I see. (*He gives the ring back to Cranmer*)
Cranmer We can't assume her guilt, sire.
Norfolk What else are we to assume? They'll confess, majesty. There'll be no doubt.

Henry looks from one to the other, in profound shock

Henry *Fidus ultra finis.* Bad Latin.
Norfolk May I take charge of the investigation, majesty? For the honour of my family.
Henry There'll be no investigation. This is all a confusion. I won't have any investigations.
Cranmer Very likely it is a confusion, sire. But it is widely reported. There is talk.
Henry Let them talk.
Cranmer I think it unwise to do nothing. It gives the appearance of weakness.

Norfolk Let the nation see your strong hand at the helm, majesty.
Henry What would you have me do?
Norfolk Justice, majesty. Swift and sure.
Cranmer Let us get to the bottom of the matter. Discreetly, of course. But let it be known that your ministers are actively pursuing the truth.
Henry The truth. That's what I want. not all these damn lies.
Norfolk The truth, majesty. Without fear or favour.

Henry looks at Norfolk and Cranmer, irresolute. Cranmer turns the ring over and over in his hands

Henry (*his eyes falling on the ring*) Very well.

Henry exits. Cranmer follows

The Captain of the King's Guard and his men take their places behind Norfolk

Katherine enters, walking with Lady Rochford

Katherine sees Norfolk, and runs to him. Norfolk stares at her coldly

Katherine Uncle! I sent word to you. We must talk.
Norfolk Indeed we must.
Katherine What's the matter, uncle?

The fury breaks through Norfolk's icy stillness

Norfolk Don't "uncle" me, madam! You will remain in your apartments in the palace until suitable quarters are found for you elsewhere. You will communicate with no-one ——
Katherine Please ... What have I done?
Norfolk Lust, madam, lust! Your juvenile debaucheries damn only your own worthless soul, but cuckold a king and you damn a kingdom.
Katherine But it's not true! I've never been unfaithful to the king.
Norfolk Take her away.

The Guards put their hands on Katherine's arms. She shakes them off

Katherine It's not true! Jane, tell them! Does the king believe this? Let me see him. Take me to the king.
Norfolk Take her away!

The Guards take hold of Katherine more forcibly now, and drag her backwards. Katherine becomes frenzied.

Katherine It's a lie! Tell the king ... I must see the king. Let me go! Who accuses me? They lie Jane, tell them! Uncle! Believe me! ——

The Guards drag Katherine off

Norfolk (*turning his icy gaze on Lady Rochford*) You have done good work today, madam.
Lady Rochford I had no choice.
Norfolk You chose to save yourself. Now join the queen in her apartments.
Lady Rochford But the queen is under arrest.
Norfolk Do as I say.

Norfolk exits

Katherine enters. She is alone, quieter now, but still trembling with fear

Cranmer enters, accompanied by William

William takes notes throughout the following

Cranmer (*respectfully*) My lady.
Katherine Does the king send for me?
Cranmer No, ma'am. The king sends to know the truth.
Katherine I've told the truth. This is a lie made up by my enemies. I've never been unfaithful to the king. Never.
Cranmer If you've been slandered, we'll find it out. But the king must know all of it, ma'am. You must understand that. Conceal anything, and the king will believe that you conceal everything.
Katherine Who accuses me? Tell me what they say. I have nothing to hide.
Cranmer Truth is truth, from whatever source.
Katherine And lies are lies, sir. The king knows I've never lied to him. Ask him.
Cranmer The king is merciful. He takes account of your youth ——
Katherine Do you think I'm so ungrateful, so unloving, so stupid, as to betray my lord the king? Do you think I don't know the consequences? The whole world knows the fate of an unfaithful queen. I would never put myself at such risk. Nor would I so wound the king. I love the king, sir. That's the truth.
Cranmer But not the only truth. You may love the king and love another too.
Katherine I have not betrayed the king. (*She weeps uncontrollably*)

Cranmer (*adopting a gentle paternal manner to Katherine*) All right. All right. Let's establish just what has taken place, one step at a time. That's what you want, and that's what the king wants. So wipe your eyes and calm yourself, and you'll come to no harm.

Katherine regains control of herself

Now — Thomas Culpeper is known to you, I think? Yes?
Katherine Yes.
Cranmer He is your friend, yes?
Katherine Yes.
Cranmer One may love one's friends, surely? Yes?
Katherine Yes.
Cranmer And you love Culpeper, yes?
Katherine As a friend, yes.
Cranmer You have spent time alone with him?
Katherine Yes.
Cranmer (*to William*) She loves him. She's been alone with him.
Katherine Is that a crime, Archbishop?
Cranmer For a young woman to be alone with a young man? No, ma'am, that is no crime, not in itself. Shall we continue?
Katherine Yes.
Cranmer This time alone with your friend was in a bedchamber, ma'am?

Katherine falters

Now we must arrive at the truth, ma'am. You say the king knows you've never lied to him. He does believe you've deceived him now. The only path now is the path of complete candour.

Katherine sees how bad it looks, and is very afraid, and wants to trust him, but hardly knows if she dare

Open your heart to me, child. Then there'll be no more of these sordid investigations. There's only one truth here, and we'll come at it in the end, but you know it now, and your nature is to be truthful. He came to your bedchamber, didn't he?
Katherine Yes.
Cranmer Because you loved him very much once, did you not?
Katherine Yes.
Cranmer And you love him still, don't you?
Katherine Yes.
Cranmer There, now. This is honesty at last.

Katherine But I've never been unfaithful to the king.

Cranmer's expression changes abruptly. He becomes angry

Cranmer What is this, madam? You've just confessed ——
Katherine I said I loved Culpeper. But he never touched me.
Cranmer Never touched you?
Katherine No, sir. Only my husband the king has that right.
Cranmer What nonsense is this? Loving but not touching?
Katherine Call it nonsense if you like. That's how it was.
Cranmer Your love belongs to the king, ma'am, and you know it as well as I do.
Katherine My body belongs to the king, and he has it. No other man has touched me since my marriage. But even the king doesn't tell me to love no-one but him. Am I not to love my family? Am I not to love my friends? Am I not to love my God?
Cranmer In a different way. These are all different forms that love may take.
Katherine As is my love for Culpeper.
Cranmer Adultery is adultery, ma'am!
Katherine Is it possible to commit adultery without touching?
Cranmer This has become ridiculous. The king will be gravely displeased.
Katherine Why? Because I've not been unfaithful to him?
Cranmer This is not the end of the matter, ma'am. We'll meet again, when you're in a more penitent frame of mind.
Katherine Tell the king what I've said, Archbishop. No more, and no less. The time will come when you'll answer to God for what you do today.

Katherine exits

Henry enters

Henry sees Cranmer, but does not acknowledge him. He walks up and down, tormented. He wants to know, and not to know, how the investigation is proceeding. Cranmer understands this very well. After a few moments, Henry turns on him

Henry You will hang about so, Cranmer. Have you nothing better to do?
Cranmer If your majesty will give me leave ——
Henry Go. For God's sake, go.

Cranmer bows and heads towards the exit

You'll keep me informed, of course.

Cranmer Of course, sire.

Henry So I take it there's nothing?

Cranmer I prefer to be sure of my ground before troubling your majesty.

Henry So you're not sure of your ground?

Cranmer I'm not yet at the bottom of the affair, sire.

Henry The affair? The accusation, you mean. The rumour.

Cranmer Just so, sire.

Henry Well, go and get on with it. Do you think I enjoy this twilight world? All things possible, and nothing certain.

Cranmer Not much longer, I think, sire.

Cranmer bows and exits, with William

Henry (*thinking aloud*) Why is it that once you let suspicion in, it fattens in the head? I do nothing to feed it. I argue with it, and prove it wrong. I discredit it. I give it no hospitality. And yet it grows fatter and fatter, and pushes at the inside of my skull, until I feel my head will burst! Dear God! What do I care for reasons of state? What do I care for bully truth itself? All I hear is a voice crying, "Let it be yesterday again. Let me be loved." Is it so much to ask?

Henry exits

Culpeper, semi-conscious and blood-stained, is dragged in by two guards

Norfolk enters

Norfolk Lift him up.

The guards haul the beaten and chained figure to his knees, where he remains, slowly recovering the strength to lift his head. Norfolk takes all this for granted and barely looks at him.

You are accused of criminal intercourse with the queen on the night of August 29th. We have proof. We have witnesses. Do you confess?

Culpeper shakes his head

Must I squeeze it out of you? Don't doubt it, sir, I will. Don't look for pity. You fouled her, sir, you rammed her, you bulled her, you stuck her, I know it, you know it, and now the time has come to pay the price.

Culpeper (*very low*) I didn't.

This obstinacy sends Norfolk into a raving fury

Norfolk Was it sweet? Did you sweat till you wet the bed? Did you hump and pump till you were hopping like a kettle, and spouting, and a-wash and a-gush with lust? I'm a man, sir, I know how it is, I've practised the slippery sport!

Culpeper I didn't do it.

Norfolk You were in her bedchamber! Do you deny it?

Culpeper I was there.

Norfolk She's fresh, she's ripe, she's tender, any man would want her. Do you deny it?

Culpeper I wanted her.

Norfolk You wanted her, and you had her.

Culpeper I never touched her.

Norfolk You ask the king to believe that? There isn't a man in the country would believe you.

Culpeper She's the queen. How could I touch her?

Norfolk You're a man. How could you not touch her?

Culpeper Are men so helpless?

Norfolk When woman lifts her skirts, man unbuttons. That is a rule of nature. And the queen is a notorious whore.

Culpeper That's a lie!

Culpeper tries to throw himself on Norfolk, but the guards restrain him; he struggles, spitting his contempt at Norfolk

Cranmer enters

Cranmer (*to Norfolk*) I see your methods of interrogation have lost none of their subtlety.

Norfolk I'm not finished with him yet.

Cranmer No confession, then?

Norfolk If your grace would be so kind as to let me complete the interrogation ——

Cranmer ignores Norfolk and speaks directly to Culpeper

Cranmer I come from the queen. She's made a full confession. She loves Thomas Culpeper. She loves you still.

Culpeper The queen said that?

Cranmer She did.

Culpeper Bring me to her. Let me hear her with my own ears.

Cranmer As proof of her love for you, she gave me this. (*He holds out the ring*)

Culpeper looks at the ring, and knows it's all over now. He bows his head

(*Reading from the ring*) *Fidus ultra finis.*
Culpeper Then it's over.
Cranmer It is.

Culpeper lifts his head high, gives up all hope, and is released

Culpeper All I have left is my little piece of eternity. I love Kate, sir. I've
loved her since I first saw her, and I'll love her to the day I die.
Norfolk (*looking at Cranmer with satisfaction*) I think we have it.
Cranmer Oh, yes. We're there now, all right.
Norfolk Take him away.

The guards lead Culpeper off

Henry enters. He proceeds to seat himself formally, as for a royal audience

Norfolk and Cranmer approach Henry and bow

Norfolk Culpeper has confessed, sire. He wriggled, but I speared him. He
is the queen's lover, sire.
Henry (*flinching*) Did you use instruments?
Norfolk No, sire. He confessed it freely.
Henry And the queen? Does she confess also?
Cranmer Yes, sire.
Henry I will not believe it till I hear it from her own mouth.
Cranmer Remember her youth, sire ——
Henry And my age? (*He turns aside, to mask a wave of pain. Then,
mastering himself*) This so-called confession. Tell me her words. What
words did she use? (*He suffers acutely as he hears the following*)
Cranmer (*producing, and referring to, William's notes*) "He came to your
bedchamber?" "Yes". "You loved him?" "Yes." "You love him still?"
"Yes."
Henry "Yes", she says. "Yes. Yes." Let me see the words.

Henry takes the notes before Cranmer can stop him and scans them

Who wrote these notes?
Cranmer My secretary, sire.
Henry She says he never touched her. She says she has not been unfaithful.
Cranmer Fear, sire. She hopes to save herself.

Henry Then why admit she loves him?

Cranmer What she says is impossible, sire. To deceive your majesty so far, and no further.

Henry What does Culpeper say? You tell me Culpeper confesses they were lovers. Do you mean, in the body? Did he confess to that?

Norfolk Not as such, sire.

Henry Didn't you ask him?

Norfolk I asked him, of course. He denies it. What else could he do, sire? His life hangs on it.

Henry He denies it. She denies it. So who affirms it?

Cranmer Common sense, sire. Human nature. The hour. The place. The secrecy.

Henry (*reading*) "My body belongs to the king". That's what she says.

Norfolk Sire, forgive me, but how can she love Culpeper and be faithful to you? The woman is a deceiving whore, sire. She's not to be believed.

Henry I loved her, Norfolk. I loved her. Can't you understand that? (*He hands back the notes. All at once he's feeling old and weak*)

Cranmer Should the council proceed to the drawing up of charges, sire?

Norfolk She's a harlot, sire. Can't have a harlot as queen. I say it though she's my own flesh and blood. I serve the king and the country, not any narrow family interest.

Henry (*waving his hands at the others, wanting to be left alone*) I told you. I must hear it from her own mouth. Send her to me.

Norfolk Sire, is that wise?

Henry Send her to me. Go away! All of you, go!

Norfolk and Cranmer bow and exit

Henry comes forward and speaks his thoughts aloud

Henry I know my Bible well. *Relinquet homo patrem et matrem suam* — a man shall leave his father and mother — *et adhaerebit uxori suae* — and cleave to his wife — *et erunt duo in carne una* — and they shall be two, in one flesh ... St Paul said the same to the Corinthians, "Know ye not that he which is joined to a harlot is one body, for two shall be one flesh." *In carne una!* Even with a harlot! They tell me she loves him, and all I see is her arms opening —— (*He flinches with the pain and turns back to his theology to escape it*) *In carne una.* Is this rhetoric, or do the words mean what they say, no more and no less? One flesh. Who are we to dispute with God and find our own meaning here, saying he speaks only of a coupling, a bonding, a symbolic fusion? Is "one flesh" a symbolic fusion? My leg is my flesh. Is it symbolically fused to me? No, *it is me!* Is it possible that by doing the deed, we become one flesh? That she with whom I do it becomes me?

Katherine enters far off, escorted by guards. She moves slowly towards Henry

(*Ever more carried away*) If so, if by this act I become her and she becomes me, then he who does this deed with my wife does it to me. He pierces me! He penetrates me! He *rapes* me!

Katherine now stands before Henry in silence. Slowly his gaze turns towards her. The sight of her seems to calm him down

(*Quietly*) Kate?
Katherine (*very frightened, knowing her life is at stake*) My lord.
Henry They say... They say such things. How could I have loved you more?
Katherine My lord ...
Henry I thought you loved me, Kate. I swear to God I thought you loved me.
Katherine I loved you, my lord.
Henry And Culpeper too?

For a long moment, she doesn't answer. Then:

Katherine Yes, my lord. But ——
Henry (*turning away, savage in his pain*) Yes! She says yes! Her own mouth says yes!
Katherine I never loved you the less in loving him.
Henry Was my love not enough for you? Was I too old? Did my body disgust you after all?
Katherine No.
Henry It disgusts me now. I have no more need of it. I cast it off me. Let it die. Let it rot.
Katherine So it will. Our bodies are not our own. Neither of us is free.
Henry (*remembering her words to him at the beginning*) Let's take each other for friends, you said. Like prisoners cast into the same jail. And if we're kind to each other, the love will come.
Katherine And so it did.
Henry And Culpeper too?
Katherine I loved him before I knew you, sir. Was I to love him the less because the king loved me too?
Henry Yes. That you were. I married you, Kate. I made you my wife.
Katherine And from that day on, I never touched another man.
Henry He came to your bedchamber. You love him. You said so.
Katherine He never touched me, nor I him.
Henry You lie! You're afraid, and you lie!
Katherine (*weeping and shaking with terror*) I am afraid, my lord, but I don't lie. Believe it, and be merciful.

Henry To Culpeper, too?
Katherine (*sinking to her knees*) Yes, my lord. I beg you. To Culpeper too.

Henry looks long on Katherine, with a heavy heart

Henry What does it matter, after all? He's there at every turn. When you look
on me with your sweet face, a voice in my ear whispers, and Culpeper too.
When you say you love me, the voice whispers, and Culpeper too. Any man
would take it hard. But the king — the king can't endure it. The law must
take its course. (*Slowly, and with finality, he turns away, sealing his
feelings within himself*)

Servants enter with Henry's robes of state

*During the following, the servants dress Henry; with each additional heavy
magnificent garment, he becomes more the king, and less the man*

Katherine Sir. I'm afraid.

Henry isn't listening

If you ever loved me, sir, pity me. Am I to die, sir? Am I to be hurt to death?
Henry (*without looking at her; his voice cold and proud*) Have you not hurt
me? I was young again with you. I was immortal. Why should you live
when I am left to die?

*Now Katherine knows there's no hope for her. She rises, her whole body
shaking with uncontrollable fear*

Katherine My youth to give you youth. My life to give you life. I have no
more to give you, my lord.

*Norfolk, Cranmer, and Wriothesley enter. Culpeper enters, guarded. Lady
Rochford enters, guarded*

*The members of the Privy Council line up, stiff and formal, on either side of
the King. The guards take up positions by Katherine*

*Culpeper openly gazes on Katherine, his head held high. He is resigned to
his death, and has passed beyond fear*

Norfolk The court of the Privy Council has heard the evidence in the case
of the queen's adultery with Thomas Culpeper. The court finds all three
accused guilty as charged.

Lady Rochford Not me! I'm not guilty! You don't mean me! (*She throws herself to her knees before Cranmer*) Tell them! You promised!

Cranmer never moves a muscle. All four men, Henry, Cranmer, Norfolk, Wriothesley, seem turned to stone

Norfolk The sentences are as follows. Lady Jane Rochford, procuress: death. Does the king assent?

Henry nods

Lady Rochford (*panicking; screaming*) No-o-o! You promised to protect me! No-o-o!

Cranmer gives a discreet sign

　　Guards drag Lady Rochford off by a side exit. She screams all the way

Norfolk Thomas Culpeper, adulterer: death. Does the king assent?

Henry nods

Culpeper's eyes are still on Katherine. He speaks for her alone

Culpeper I'll be waiting.

Guards lead Culpeper away. Katherine's eyes follow him. She can't speak for fear

Norfolk Katherine Howard, adulteress: death. Does the king assent?

Henry looks at Katherine, and sees that her eyes are still on Culpeper

　　Culpeper looks back one last time and exits

Like a statue cracking, Henry nods

　　Guards lead Katherine away. She is so weakened by terror that she has to be helped as she walks

A moment of silence. Then:

Cranmer Justice is done.

All Long live the king!

Cranmer, Norfolk, Wriothesley and the rest file off

Henry is left, a lone figure, at the front of the stage

Henry (*speaking his thoughts aloud*) Long live the king? No, not long. What right have they to youth, when the king is old? What right have they to love, when the king is alone? What right has the sun to set, when the king needs light?

The curtains open on the pavilion and the Lights come up to reveal Katherine, standing before the execution block. She gazes at it, motionless. Then she kneels before it, and very slowly lowers her head

Distant drum-beats signify the approaching execution. Night begins to fall

Henry stands gazing at the audience, filled with a weary self-knowledge

Yes, yes, yes, the fat old monster with the stinking leg is a mockery of a man, I know. The fool in his folly commands the sun not to set, because he fears the night. But still the darkness comes. How pitiful he is, how lacking in dignity, with his britches bursting open under the sag of his gut, and all his private vices showing. All that envy, all that littleness of spirit. Do you think I don't know? Do you think I'm not ashamed? But old men outlive their pride. We learn cunning, we have no scruples, we feel no pity. Anything to delay the coming of the night.

Katherine lays her head at last upon the block, as if to sleep. Darkness descends over her. The distant drums fall silent. Only Henry is left, in the glimmer of departing day

Silence. So it's over, then. My sweet bird is free. How is it with you, Kate? Is it sunrise, where you are? Now you'll be young for ever. You have me to thank for that. I loved you, and I believed you loved me. But then you broke my heart, and that was unkind. I'm old, you see. As old as God. He too wanted to be loved for Himself, and so He made us free, and gave us the power to reject His love. And possessing that power, we use it, and God is not loved. What can be done, will be done. There will be cruelty, and injustice, and hatred, and war. And God, who wanted love so much, sees His creation turned to pain. And so He looks away, in His greatness, in His loneliness, and darkness falls about Him, and He says — nothing.

The last of the Light fades into darkness

CURTAIN

FURNITURE AND PROPERTY LIST

ACT I

Off stage: Candles (**Servants**)
Candle (**Katherine**)
Candle (**Katherine**)
Gown (**Maidservants**)
Henry's robes of state (**Servants**)
Two royal capes (**Servants**)

Personal: **Captain of the Guard**: sword
Culpeper: ring
Cranmer: ring

During Lighting change on p.1

Set: BEHIND PAVILION CURTAINS: Royal bed

ACT II

Set: ON ROYAL BED: **Katherine**'s night clothes

Off stage: Candle (**Servant**)
Notepaper, pen (**William**)

Personal: **Cranmer: William**'s notes

After curtains close on pavilion p. 46

Strike: Royal bed

Set: BEHIND PAVILION CURTAINS: Execution block

LIGHTING PLOT

Practical fittings required: nil
Open stage with curtained area US. The same throughout

ACT I

To open: Darkness

Cue 1	Procession enters *Bring up lights inside pavilion and covering glow on candles*	(Page 1)
Cue 2	**Henry** and **Culpeper** exit *Fade lights in pavilion and covering glow*	(Page 1)
Cue 3	Fanfare *Bring up lights inside pavilion and on whole stage*	(Page 1)
Cue 4	Pavilion curtains close *Fade pavilion lights*	(Page 3)
Cue 5	Procession exits *Fade lights on whole stage to night setting*	(Page 3)
Cue 6	**Katherine** enters *Bring up covering glow on candle*	(Page 3)
Cue 7	**Culpeper** blows out the candle *Cut covering glow*	(Page 3)
Cue 8	**Lady Rochford** enters *Bring up covering glow on candle*	(Page 4)
Cue 9	**Lady Rochford** lights **Katherine**'s candle *Slightly increase covering glow*	(Page 4)
Cue 10	**Lady Rochford** exits *Decrease covering candle glow*	(Page 5)
Cue 11	**Katherine** and **Culpeper** exit, arm in arm *Bring up lights to early morning setting*	(Page 6)

Cue 12	Pavilion curtains open *Bring up lights in pavilion*	(Page 6)
Cue 13	**Anne**, **Lady Rochford** and **Katherine** exit *Fade lights in pavilion*	(Page 10)
Cue 14	**Norfolk** exits *Dim lights to dusk during the following*	(Page 27)
Cue 15	**Anne** and **Katherine** enter *Bring up lights to daytime setting*	(Page 30)
Cue 16	The procession re-forms *Bring up bright lights far* us	(Page 35)

ACT II

Cue 17	Music *Bring up lights on whole stage*	(Page 36)
Cue 18	**Lady Rochford** and **Norfolk** exit *Fade lights to night setting*	(Page 37)
*Cue*19	**Henry** enters with a servant with a candle *Bring up covering glow on candle*	(Page 38)
Cue 20	**Henry** blows out the candle *Cut covering glow on candle*	(Page 39)
Cue 21	**Henry** and **Katherine** exit *Brighten lights to daytime setting*	(Page 39)
Cue 22	**Katherine** and a **maidservant** enter *Bring up lights in pavilion*	(Page 43)
Cue 23	**Katherine** exits; the pavilion curtains close *Fade pavilion lights*	(Page 46)
Cue 24	The pavilion curtains open *Bring up lights in pavilion; fade lights elsewhere except on* **Henry**	(Page 67)
Cue 25	**Katherine** lays her head on the block *Fade lights on pavilion; slowly fade lights on **Henry** during the following*	(Page 67)
Cue 26	**Henry**: " ... he says — nothing." *Fade to black-out*	(Page 67)

EFFECTS PLOT

ACT I

ACT II